THE VILLAGES OF EAST YORKSHIRE

Martin Limon

BLACKTHORN PRESS

Blackthorn Press, Blackthorn House
Middleton Rd, Pickering YO18 8AL
United Kingdom

www.blackthornpress.com

ISBN 978 1 906259 25 9

© Martin Limon 2010

CONTENTS

Introduction
Preface

INTRODUCTION

The East Riding of Yorkshire is one of the most rural of English counties, with a population of 314,000 in 2001, excluding Hull, the county's only city, which has a population of 244,000. Outside of Hull, life takes place in small towns and villages some of which are set in the rolling landscape of the Yorkshire Wolds and others in the flatter more low-lying parts of the county like Holderness. Many of the back roads are little changed since medieval times with just a coat of tarmac to remind the driver that he is in the twenty-first century.

Many East Yorkshire villages have Anglian origins.

Agriculture dominated the lives of the population from prehistoric times to the beginnings of the industrial revolution. The ruling classes might change, from Roman to Angle, to Dane to Norman to rich industrialist moving out of Hull, who would often buy the manor house and title of 'Lord of the Manor' but for the majority of the population, the care of the land and its animals were of prime importance. Even those not directly engaged in tending the land were dependent on it, providing the services of blacksmith, landlord, shopkeeper, miller or priest.

The village church, as at here in Nafferton, dominated the medieval village.

The church provided some spiritual guidance and a rudimentary education in some villages and the landscape is still dominated by spire and tower, although attendances have fallen, as alternatives to spending Sundays appear more attractive. The parish was the immediate centre of law and custom with only occasional reference to the higher authorities of County or Parliament when the need arose.

Although the 'Black Death' of the fourteenth century, shook this system, with some villages being deserted, it was the agricultural revolution of the eighteenth century, which brought the first major changes to village life. As late as 1771, Arthur Young could still describe the East Riding as containing "far more open field than enclosure" but by 1815 the greater part of the East Riding had been enclosed. The chief landowners had Acts of Parliament drawn up which redistributed the medieval strips of land into compact farms where the new farming methods could be introduced. The increased agricultural production meant profits for some but many of the poorer inhabitants were deprived of their stake in the land and were reduced to farm labourers, working for a wage or their keep. When times were bad, the Workhouse with its hated rules was the last resort. Enclosure changed the social mix of the village with the larger landowners moving out to purpose built farms, surrounded by their land while the village itself was left to the farm labourers and village craftsmen.

With the Industrial Revolution in the eighteenth and nineteenth century, alternatives to farm work sprang up. Many moved to the towns and cities to work in the factories and the rural population began to decline. Some villages and towns had their own small-scale units of production, which provided some work for villagers and immigrant labourers. There was a change in social attitudes too and by 1850 farmers who had eaten the same kind of food and wore the same kind of clothes as the poorer folk and thought the same thoughts and talked in the same dialect, now felt themselves socially superior and began to pay their labourers a weekly wage and the custom of labourers living on the farm declined. The influx of newcomers in the twentieth century in search of cheaper housing and a rural lifestyle brought many benefits but saw the end of the tight social and economic units which had existed for centuries.

The coming of the railways from around 1840, which gradually connected the villages of East Yorkshire to the towns and cities, meant it was possible to commute to work or send produce greater distances. The railway was largely replaced by motor transport after the cuts of the 1960s but the pattern of commuting and the possibility of running enterprises out of villages persists.

The impact of the First World War and, to a lesser extent the Second, can be seen from the many war memorials to be found in every village, such as at Cottingham (left). Young men were plucked out of their village lives to die on the battlefields of France. Those who survived were shown a wider world and many became politically active, determined to end the old order of things. This, combined with the spread of universal education after 1870 meant broader horizons and opportunities for some.

Horses continued to provide most of the power on farms until well into the 1940s.

Although still of prime importance, agriculture no longer employs the numbers it did and the villagers of East Yorkshire now earn their livings in a variety of ways which would have astonished their forbears. They are better fed, housed, educated and entertained than ever before but the landscape they live in remains rural and the need for community in a rapidly changing world persists.

In this new book, Martin Limon fills in this broad sweep of historical trends with the individual record of village life in East Yorkshire, examining the history of forty East Yorkshire villages and the characters who worked the fields and workshops and prayed in the churches and drank in the ale-houses, many of which still stand and invite the traveller to stop and stare and remember.

Alan Avery

PREFACE

Early in 2007 Roy Woodcock, the editor of 'The Journal' a Yorkshire county magazine based in Hull, asked me if I would be interested in writing a series called 'village visit'. I eagerly accepted the challenge and decided from the outset that I would focus my attention on social history, personalities, and interesting events to make the series as accessible as possible to the readership of the magazine. Much of the research was carried out at the 'Treasure House' in Beverley where the East Riding Archive's collection of historical records, old newspapers, census returns and the like provided a rich source of inspiration for a series that is now in its fourth year of publication.

I would like to take this opportunity to thank the staff of the East Riding Archive for their unstinting assistance and advice in providing me with the 'raw materials' for many hours of enjoyable research. My thanks also go the History Press for their permission to use extracts from 'Tales from the East Riding' and 'More Tales from the East Riding' in some village studies.

With around four hundred East Riding villages to choose from any book like this has to be selective but since the 'village visit' series is ongoing I hope to cover many others in due course. Some of the villages early in the Journal series, like Walkington, Swanland and Kilham, appeared in my book 'More Tales from the East Riding' but included in this volume are forty more drawn from many parts of East Yorkshire.

Martin Limon

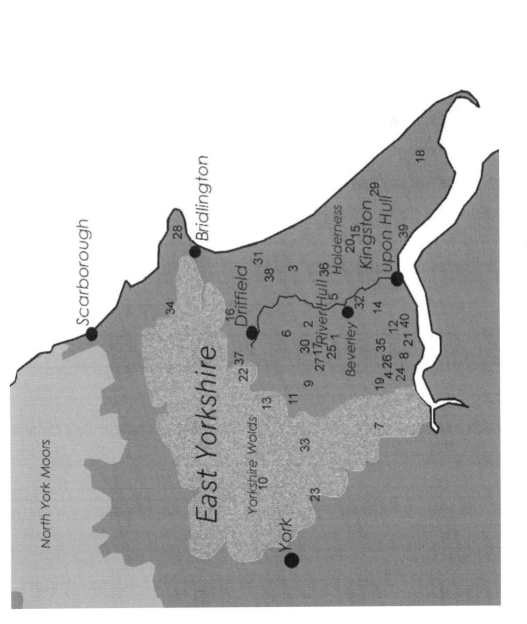

1. Bishop Burton
2. Lockington
3. Brandesburton
4. South Cave
5. Tickton
6. Hutton Cranswick
7. Holme-upon-Spalding Moor
8. Brough
9. Middleton-on-the-Wolds
10. Stamford Bridge
11. Warter
12. Kirkella
13. Huggate
14. Cottingham
15. Sproatley
16. Nafferton
17. Leconfield
18. Patrington
19. North Cave
20. Skirlaugh
21. North Ferriby
22. Wetwang
23. Sutton-upon-Derwent
24. Ellerker
25. Cherry Burton
26. Brantingham
27. Etton
28. Flamborough
29. Burton Pidsea
30. Lund
31. Skipsea
32. Woodmansey
33. Barmby Moor
34. Wold Newton
35. Little Weighton
36. Leven
37. Garton-on-the-Wolds
38. Beeford
39. Paull
40. Anlaby

CHAPTER 1

BISHOP BURTON

Situated in a sheltered hollow astride the A1079 road from Beverley to York, Bishop Burton has long been regarded as a picture-book English village with its neat whitewashed cottages, two village ponds, a charming church and an unhurried pace of life. The unique appeal of the place has long been recognised by visitors to the area. Back in 1892 a local directory stated: "it is the proud boast of the inhabitants that Bishop Burton is the prettiest village in the East Riding and it must be conceded that it has very good claims to this distinction." The power of the village to fascinate newcomers has not faded in the years since then and in 1939 Bishop Burton was judged to be one of the twelve most-lovely villages in the whole of England. Many of today's drivers passing through the village, their natural caution reinforced by the frequent presence of a mobile speed camera, only gain a brief impression of the beauty of the place. A much better way to appreciate the charms of the village is to linger awhile and explore its ancient streets on foot.

Although the word Burh-ton (meaning a fortified village or farmstead) came from the Angles, a Germanic tribe who settled in the area from the fifth century, the origins of Bishop Burton are in fact much older. As well as prehistoric burial mounds other finds suggest a Roman presence for in 1721 it was claimed that two mosaic floors from a Roman villa were discovered and in 1892 Roman coins were unearthed on the site of the present day Bishop Burton College. The name Bishop Burton only appeared in the 13th century and came about because of its association with the Archbishops of York who had a manor house here.

Exploring the Bishop Burton of today provides other clues on the history of the village especially a wealth of distinctive street names like Callas, Pudding Gate, Joby Lane, Rattan Row and Finkle Street. Although it cannot be proved conclusively, some of these street signs (like Finkle Street and Pudding Gate) suggest a Scandinavian influence on the village in the period before the Norman Conquest of 1066. The word gate is sometimes derived from the old Norse word gata meaning way, street or road while pudding probably refers to a surface of rounded pebbles, naturally cemented together, rather than any culinary meaning. Callas is another interesting street name and most likely reflects Bishop Burton's

1

The second of the village ponds with one of Bishop Burton's beautiful 18th century houses.

links with the wool trade of the Middle Ages when Calais merchants had a monopoly of wool sales to European customers. Those who explore the village will also find a Mill Lane leading to the remains of the windmill where in 1857 William Watson worked grinding corn into flour. The sails of the windmill were removed in 1895 but the stump of its tower, now embodied in a private house, can still be seen. Another highlight of any village exploration is All Saint's Church, originally founded by St John of Beverley early in the eighth century but which underwent considerable renovation in the nineteenth.

Probably the most famous of Bishop Burton's many signs linking the present with the past is that of the 'Altisidora' public house. In the 18th and 19th centuries Yorkshire was a major centre of horse breeding and through the efforts of Richard Watt (1786-1855) Bishop Burton became famous for the quality of its bloodstock. Watt was the son of a wealthy Liverpool merchant who, in 1783, had purchased the High Hall at Bishop Burton. Watt's horses and harlequin racing colours brought fame to the village, a fact reflected in the various names given to Bishop Burton's public house in the early nineteenth century. In a directory of 1823 it was called 'Evander' after one of Richard Watt's horses; later it became the 'Horse and Jockey' and finally the 'Altisidora'. In 1813 'Altisidora' had become the first of Richard Watt's horses to win the England's premier horse race of that time: the St Ledger. Watt went on to win three more St Ledgers between 1823 and 1833 with horses called 'Barefoot', 'Memnon' and 'Rockingham'. After they died many of his horses, including 'Altisidora', were buried beneath the parkland surrounding the High Hall with their graves being marked by oak trees. Following the death of Richard Watt his son William carried on the business. Today, the Bishop Burton connection with horse racing is kept alive by a bequest of £3,000 to the trustees of Beverley Racecourse to fund the yearly Watt Memorial Race.

Over the years this beautiful and seemingly tranquil village has seen its share of scandal, violence and tragedy and these stories were reported in local newspapers of the time. In January 1900, at a time when divorce was both unusual and costly, John Smith: a stud groom working at Bishop Burton began proceedings against his wife for adultery with Arthur Whipp a farmer's son of Mountain Pleasant Farm. After letters and a confession from Smith's wife were read and witnesses were heard the court granted the divorce with damages of £100 being awarded against Whipp.

Bishop Burton High Hall.

In 1909 the village was again the centre of unwelcome attention after a violent death at harvest time. On Sunday 19th September many farm labourers engaged in gathering in the harvest at farms around Bishop Burton were drinking heavily at the Altisidora Public House. A drink-fuelled argument had erupted between them and subsequently one labourer (Edward Dunn) had been found dead in the road about a mile from the village. At an inquest it was said that Dunn had died from a fractured skull after falling onto the road during a sustained assault. After some confusion among the authorities and the police as to who was responsible for Dunn's death Harry Gillbank of Lings Farm at Bishop Burton was charged with murder and was committed to stand trial at the York Assizes in November 1909. In the event Gillbank was a very fortunate individual for the court decided that a murder charge was inappropriate in the circumstances and when the Grand Jury refused to try him on a lesser charge of manslaughter he was released from custody. The judge, Mr Justice Bucknill speaking on *November* 20th 1909 said he was "unable to understand why the magistrates at Beverley had committed the accused for trial on the capital charge" and declared, "it was the most extraordinary case he had ever heard during twelve years on

Bishop Burton in the 1940s.

the Bench." One outcome of the case however was that the 'Altisidora' lost its seven-day drinks licence.

These days one of Bishop Burton's major claims to fame is that it is home to Britain's leading land-based college. In 1951 the East Riding County Council bought the High Hall at Bishop Burton and demolished it to make way for an 'Institute of Agriculture'. The project was the inspiration of Sir John Dunnington-Jefferson, a County Councillor, who questioned the financial wisdom of paying grants to East Riding folk to attend West Riding colleges when the county could have its own. The Institute first opened its doors in September 1954 with a mere forty students and only two courses: a National Certificate in Agriculture and a Certificate in Rural Home Management. These days there are more than 3000 students and 470 staff on a 1000 acre site with a range of courses to degree level including agriculture, countryside and environmental management, garden design and equine management. In fifty years the college has risen from humble beginning to become Britain's only centre

Bishop Burton College.

of excellence for agriculture and equine studies. The success of Bishop Burton College looks likely to continue into the future and since 2006 huge sums have been spent to create a modern state-of-the-art campus. These new facilities include a new equine indoor arena, a dog-grooming centre, a new sports hall and improved residential accommodation for students.

The College also helps to perpetuate the rural feel of Bishop Burton; unlike many other settlements in the East Riding the village has not seen a large-scale development of new houses. Open spaces like the village greens and pasture-land within the heart of the village add to this feeling of rural tranquillity and explain Bishop Burton's enduring appeal to those who work in Hull or Beverley.

Anyone who drives into Bishop Burton from the direction of Beverley today and sees the magical vista of the Mere (front cover) come into view cannot fail to be captivated by the beauty of the village. Though the county may have a wealth of lovely rural communities for sheer visual splendour Bishop Burton must represent the jewel in East Yorkshire's crown.

CHAPTER 2

LOCKINGTON

Although the East Riding contains a wealth of beautiful villages the appeal of several of them has been spoilt in recent times by the growth in traffic especially when a main road cuts through them. The village of Lockington, six miles north-west of Beverley, is different because it does not lie on a major trunk road but is situated midway between the A164 route and the B1248. Protected by a conservation area since 1974, Lockington is a very pretty village with its character strongly influenced by the Bryan Mills Beck that runs through it and is crossed by several fords and a road bridge.

Like many places in the East Riding the origins of Lockington can be traced back to Anglo-Saxon times for the name is thought to be derived from 'Loca's farm'. It seems likely that Loca was an Anglian chieftain who arrived in East Yorkshire during the fifth century after the departure of the Romans. In 1893 during restoration work on the village church a brooch dated to around 500AD was found together with a number of skeletons that were buried north to south suggesting they were pagans. Although the site may long have been a place of spiritual significance it was not until the early twelfth century that a stone-built Christian church was erected there. At the time of the Domesday Book (1086) 'Locheton', as it was then known, had a mill but there was no mention of a church.

In the centuries that followed St Mary's Church would have continued to serve the spiritual needs of the villagers but Lockington was not immune to the religious controversies that affected England in the time of the Tudors and the Stuarts. One of these controversies occurred during the reign of Henry the Eighth with the king's decision to make himself head of the Church and to close the monasteries. In Yorkshire these actions were deeply resented and led to the rebellion known as the 'Pilgrimage of Grace' in 1536. One of its leaders was Sir Francis Bigod, lord of the manor of Lockington and he was one of many who were executed for treason by a vengeful king.

In the mid seventeenth century it was the turn of the vicar of Lockington, Robert Remington, to suffer for his beliefs. After the execution of King Charles the First in 1649 many 'royalist' clergy were deprived of their church livings since their loyalty to the new republican

The ford at Lockington.

regime was suspect. Remington, a royalist, had been the vicar of Lockington since 1638 but was now expelled in favour of his nephew. It was not until 1662 that he was allowed to resume his position with the restoration of the monarchy under Charles the Second.

Religious intolerance continued too under the restored monarchy with one target of persecution being the Quakers. In 1666 a group of them had assembled at a house in Lockington "to worship God in spirit and in truth" when their meeting was disrupted by Thomas Brownbrigg, the constable and others "who violently entered the house, exceedingly abused them" and then drove them from the village. When local administration and policing depended on unpaid constables such violence was not unusual and others too suffered from the harsh penal code of the time. The whipping of vagrants was sanctioned by law and from local records we learn that in July 1650 Richard Leake, one of Lockington's constables, had found William Beilby "an old man of sixty years or thereabouts" wandering and begging in the village. Accordingly he was arrested and "then and there whipped according to ye statute."

By the eighteenth century Lockington was caught up in the same changes taking place elsewhere in the East Riding. From Around 1730 the Hotham family of South Dalton became the major landowners in the village and began replacing the old mud, chalk and thatch covered dwellings with those built of brick and tile. Under the pressure of a growing population farming also changed with enclosed farms replacing the commons and open fields with their inefficient system of strip farming. This process was completed in 1772 when the Lockington Enclosure Act was passed and the pattern of fields and farms of today became established. In a directory of 1823 thirteen farmers were mentioned and they would have employed many others to carry out the labour-intensive work of the time. The village also supported two carpenters, two shoemakers, a tailor, a blacksmith and a corn miller. It was usual for a trade to be passed from father to son and, for example a directory of 1857 shows that William Ireland was the village blacksmith while thirty-five years later the skills of shoeing horses and repairing farm implements were being practised by John Ireland.

Like many villages in East Yorkshire it was the Church of England that dominated the provision of an elementary education in the basics of reading, writing and arithmetic in the nineteenth century. It was their 'National Society for the Education of the Poor' that built a new school in the village in 1844. Originally there was only one classroom although a second was added in 1875, five years after an Education Act

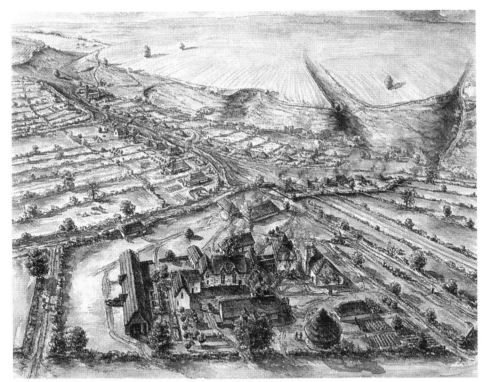
A village surrounded by its open fields before enclosure.

had made elementary education compulsory for all children. The school log book for Lockington makes interesting reading and records such things as extra holidays to mark Lockington Feast Day on the last Friday in May or poor attendance figures caused by events like haymaking or Hull Fair. In the rural economy of the time children were a vital part of the labour force at harvest time and could be the victims of accidents as much as adult workers. From a local newspaper we learn of one such incident in July 1887 when James Hanson of Lockington, age five, fell from a hay wagon when the horses pulling it gave a "sudden start". He was picked up unconscious from the road and remained that way for the rest of the day after suffering head and neck injuries.

While horse-drawn transport remained the mainstay of the village until the twentieth century the coming of the railways did at least help Lockington become less isolated. When the Hull and Bridlington railway opened in October 1846 the line passed through places like Arram and Cranswick with stations conveniently located for the villagers. This was not the case, however, with Lockington for the station lay two miles east of the village itself. It is not surprising that when economies were needed

A view of Lockington around 1900. On the left is the beck and on the right the 'Rockingham' public house. Waiting outside the village post office is a horse and trap. Note the unmade roads in the days before tarmac.

on the Hull to Bridlington route in the 1960s Lockington Station was the first to close on 13th June 1960. Yet despite its inconvenient location, it was well used by the villagers and in 1911 the stationmaster issued 9,131 tickets for journeys north to Driffield and Bridlington and south to Hull. Yet working at one of the sleepiest stations on the line was not without incident and from a local newspaper we learn that in May 1898 the stationmaster, Charles Holt, had to deal with a 25 year old Hull man intent on killing himself by climbing down onto the rails. George Rhind, an unemployed cooper who had walked out into the countryside looking for work, was charged at Beverley with the offence of trying to commit suicide. At this hearing he was declared to be insane and was sent to the East Riding Lunatic Asylum at Walkington. Two years later, in December 1900, Mr Holt was once more in the news when he collapsed at the station, and later died, after an attack of apoplexy (probably a heart attack or a stroke).

The former Lockington Railway Station on the Hull to Bridlington line. The station was two miles from the village and closed in June 1960.

In more recent times Lockington became associated with one of the worst railway accidents ever to occur in East Yorkshire. Twenty-six years after the closure of Lockington Station the location made national headlines following a terrible train crash. On the 26th July 1986 the 9.33am Bridlington to Hull train hit a van on the un-gated level crossing near to the station and was derailed. The 'lights-only' crossing had replaced manually operated gates six-months earlier as part of economy measures to stop the line from being closed. The front coach of the train overturned, the second ended up on the opposite track and the others were derailed leaving nine people dead and fifty-nine injured. The subsequent enquiry into the Lockington Rail Crash found that the signals had been working correctly and that the van driver had driven onto the crossing by mistake. It also raised serious issues about the safety of this type of remotely monitored level crossing with the result that it was decided to install barriers at all crossings on the line by the end of 1988.

Fourteen years later Lockington was to make the headlines again after a disastrous fire destroyed its primary school. A new school had replaced the old National School, which became the village hall, in 1964 but on April 8th 2000 it was destroyed during an arson attack. Two fourteen-year olds subsequently pleaded guilty to the crime and were sentenced to six months detention. Putting right the destruction they caused however took much longer and it was not until January 2002 that the rebuilt school opened its doors to pupils. Appropriately the emblem chosen for the new school uniform was a phoenix.

In the hundred years between 1901 and 2001 the population of Lockington only grew from 471 people to 542 although the beauty of the place with its quaint cottages and narrow tree lined lanes has served as a magnet for those seeking an idyllic rural location in which to live. Today the village of Lockington remains one of the most attractive locations in East Yorkshire. Its position away from the busy A164 road between Beverley and Driffield, while inconvenient to villagers having to walk to the main road to catch the bus, does at least help Lockington to retain the same rural calm of a century ago.

CHAPTER 3

BRANDESBURTON

Those who regularly explore the roads around the pretty village of Brandesburton, six miles west of Hornsea, will probably have noticed the number of lakes that are so much a feature of this part of East Yorkshire. In fact, these waters are the man-made legacy of the once thriving industry of the extraction of gravel. Brandesburton was in the fortunate position of being surrounded by a chain of gravel mounds and deposits (the terminal moraine of the North Sea ice sheet). A directory of 1892 recorded:

> "A ridge of gravel and sand runs through the centre of the parish and is known as Brandesburton Barfe. It has long served the inhabitants with gravel for the repair of the roads."

With the rise of motor transport in the early twentieth century the need for road improvements, such as the laying of tarmac surfaces, became necessary and the commercial exploitation of these gravel deposits began from the 1920s. Anyone who has seen Brandesburton's main street with its narrow L-shaped bend will understand why the village got its first bypass, as early as 1925, to assist in the development of this new industry and the movement of gravel.

Road transport has long been the key to Brandesburton's growth for in the 1820s a local directory said:

> "This extensive and populous village is pleasantly situated on the road leading from Hull to Scarborough from which places coaches and other vehicles are passing and re-passing daily which greatly tends to the benefit of its inhabitants. There are two good inns for the accommodation of travellers"

The two inns in question were the 'Cross Keys', which was renamed the 'Dacre Arms' by 1872 and the 'Black Swan'. The 'Cross Keys' was once one of the most important posting stations in the East Riding with stabling for fifty horses around a cobbled yard. An inn has stood on the site since the 16th century although the present structure dates

14

Two buses wait at the Black Swan Inn, Brandesburton around 1903. (old postcard courtesy of Beverley Local Studies Library)

from 1806. During the 19th century a room here served as the courtroom of local magistrates.

The 'Black Swan' stands in the most picturesque part of Brandesburton and dates from the mid 18th century. It too had extensive stabling and at a time when the village still had a weekly market its position next to the small green where this was held would have ensured a lively trade. Brandesburton's ancient market cross, defaced by village vandals of long ago, still marks the spot.

Brandesburton had been granted the right to hold a market and an annual fair as early as 1286 and these apparently were still prosperous in the early nineteenth century. The writer Edward Baines wrote in 1823:

> "A market for all sorts of cattle is held on alternate Wednesdays, which is very full attended, a sure criterion of its rising prosperity."

In fact Baines was mistaken for the markets and fairs were soon to disappear as Brandesburton became the victim of competition from the railways. The opening of the Hull to Bridlington railway in 1846 led to a rapid decline in the coaching trade and since the village was many miles from a station its prosperity suffered. This was a situation that one of Brandesburton's most interesting characters of the late nineteenth century, Major James Harrison of Brandesburton Hall, was determined to put right. Harrison was a prime mover in a new light railway scheme proposed in 1897 to link Beverley and North Frodingham with a station at Brandesburton to serve the needs of local people. In the event the problem of raising money for the scheme meant that the North Holderness Light Railway was never built and the village had to make do instead with a motorbus service that began in September 1903.

Squire Harrison was in many ways a controversial figure for he was also the man behind the famous 'Brandesburton Pygmies'. Harrison was a big game hunter whose trips to the Belgian Congo (modern day Zaire) brought him into contact with the smallest people in Africa: the pygmies of the Ituri Forest. Harrison saw the commercial possibilities of exhibiting the pygmies as a kind of music-hall act in Britain and despite the disapproval of the scheme by the British Foreign Secretary Lord Lansdowne, he was allowed to bring six pygmies into the country in June 1905. Reviled by some as a dwarf impresario Harrison arranged for the appearance of the pygmies at venues throughout Britain and Europe. In August 1905 he put them on show at Brandesburton Hall to a paying

Studio photograph by W.N. Downey of the 'Brandesburton Pygmies' as they appeared on stage.

audience of three thousand people and they also appeared on stage at Beverley, Driffield, Hull and Bridlington. The pygmies stayed in Britain for two years and between 'performances' they roamed free around the

James Harrison and his wife in the grounds of Brandesburton Hall. Harrison was a cricket enthusiast and during his lifetime the lawn at Brandesburton Hall was used for cricket matches. (Image courtesy of Beverley Local Studies Library)

grounds of Brandesburton Hall building shelters and hunting birds and rabbits. They were a familiar sight at the village forge where the blacksmith watched them turn horseshoe nails into arrowheads.

Harrison continued to live at Brandesburton Hall and to add to the buildings there inherited from his father. The two hundred acres of parkland surrounding it contained many exotic trees and plants gleaned from his travels abroad while a directory of the time records that the hall housed "a splendid collection of rare birds, game etc shot by Mr Harrison during his travels in Africa and America"

After the death of James Harrison Brandesburton Hall became a mental hospital (1932 to 1995) with the main house, a stable block and new buildings providing accommodation for one hundred and ninety two patients (1937). In fact Brandesburton Hospital was not the area's first example of the care of the mentally ill for a hundred years earlier there had been a private asylum at Moor Cottage (1821-1851) close to the village. Plans in the East Riding Archive in Beverley, dated September 29th 1828, show a large institution with separate day rooms for men and

Brandesburton Hall.

women, sleeping accommodation on the upper floors and airing courts for the patients as fresh air and exercise were seen as an important part of the treatment.

Reports from visiting magistrates who supervised the running of the asylum make fascinating reading with frequent references to the very excited state of the inmates especially in hot weather. Since Moor Cottage was a private asylum and had been created to make money for its owners, the Beal Family, the care of the inmates had to be paid for, sometimes by reluctant parish authorities in the East Riding. In May 1836 the magistrates received representations from the Overseers of the Poor of Foston-on-the-Wolds asking for the discharge from the asylum of Jacob Ibotson. However the magistrates declined to do so after listening to the views of a visiting surgeon who considered Ibotson to be "a dangerous idiot and an improper person to be at liberty." Yet, at a time when mental illness was not properly understood, it seems that Ibotson's incarceration at the Moor Cottage Ayslum was due only to epileptic fits.

The opening and continuing expansion of Brandesburton Hospital from the 1930s helped to swell the population of the village and this grew from five hundred and sixty eight people in 1931 to one thousand and eleven people in 1951. This upward trend in population growth also continued in the 1980s with Brandesburton becoming a dormitory village for Hull and Beverley with much new house building.

In the meantime many of Brandesburton's newer enterprises have come about with the end of gravel extraction on some sites close to the village. The lakes that comprise the water-filled former workings of Hoveringham Gravel Ltd have been used to establish leisure industries like Billabong Water Sports (1980), the Fosse Hill Jet Ski Centre (1987) and the Dacre Lakeside Park (1984). The latter began life as a touring caravan park set around a six-acre lake used for windsurfing, sailing, canoeing and fishing.

By adapting to changing circumstances therefore Brandesburton has remained a thriving community into the 21st century. At the heart of this ancient community a conservation area (1977) has protected its older buildings while former scars on the landscape created by the quarries of the past have been turned into beautiful lakeside amenities for the future.

CHAPTER 4

SOUTH CAVE

For those East Riding folk who regularly use the 'High Hunsley' route to reach the M62 motorway the village of South Cave will probably be familiar since it provides an alternative to the busy A63 corridor. Communications have in fact long been the key to the importance of the place for South Cave lay on the important Roman road from Petuaria (Brough) via Market Weighton to York and beyond. In later times an east-west route from Hull to Leeds crossed the line of the old Roman road and helps to explain the development of South Cave as a market village at the junction of the two.

Today's motorists 'dropping down' into South Cave along the A1034 might be forgiven for thinking that the area of the Market Place (dominated by an impressive town hall) has always been at the heart of this ancient settlement. In fact the origins of South Cave are to be found further to the west in the area of All Saints Church, St Helen's Well and Cave Castle. The village has existed since at least the time of the Domesday Book (1086) and is probably much older while the name 'South Cave' is thought to be derived from the Old English word caf meaning swift or quick and probably refers to the beck that runs through the village from east to west.

The status of South Cave as a market village dates back to the early Middle Ages and in 1291 Edward the First granted a charter for a market on a Monday each week and a four-day fair every year.

South Cave is a typical example of the strip farming which was common to most of East Yorkshire, where sheep rearing did not dominate. By the end of the seventeenth century the possessions of a man living there were described as:

"One [strip] Milbut Headland, one Carr Daile, one Broad Rangham, one Narrow Rangham, one North Wrangland, one Broad Santon Land, one Narrow Santon Land, one Becktoft, two Beane lands, one Broad Moore land, one Hammer land, one Skell land, one other land beyond Coney Garth, one other land called a Greengate Moorland in the Newfield, one Arras dale, in the same field; one Land within the Newfield Gates, one Lynne Butt, one high Howdale, one Low Howdale, one fracrow, one Land under

21

Cave Castle was built by Henry Barnard in 1804.

Raven flat side, one Land on the North Wold, on the Daile Side, one Wandale, one land at Moungy Nooke, one acre of Meadow lying in a certain place called the South Cave Inggs; also all that Moyety, or half, of 2 acres of meadow or pasture ground lying within South Cave field."

This was a substantial holding and the unnamed farmer would also have had rights in the common land so that when South Cave had its Act of Enclosure, he would have received a compact farm where new methods of farming, breeding and crops could be introduced.

New methods brought prosperity for some and this is indicated in South Cave by the fact that in 1796 a purpose-built market hall (now the Town Hall) was constructed by Henry Barnard the principal landowner of the parish who lived at Cave Castle. The journalist Edward Baines reported on the continuing prosperity of this market in the 1820s when he wrote:

" A great quantity of wheat is sold and sent by the Humber and its branches to Leeds, Wakefield and other populous towns of the West Riding."

The village directory of South Cave of that time also recorded the presence of Robert Sharp, teacher, whose schoolroom formed the upper floor of the new Market Hall. Robert Sharp was also a prolific writer and his diaries and letters (held by the East Riding Archive and published in 1997) provide an important account of South Cave village life in the early nineteenth century.

Robert Sharp (1773-1843) had been born at Barmston near Bridlington and in 1804 successfully applied for the job of schoolmaster at South Cave. His diaries provide us with a fascinating wealth of information about the village, its inhabitants and about South Cave's weekly market and the annual 'Cave Fair'. On the 11th June 1832 for example he wrote:

"I think I never saw more pot carts at the Market than there were today and seldom more fighting both with men and women all drunk alike. One girl who broke another man's pots was knocked down and hurt."

The Market Place at South Cave and the Town Hall.

Although with the coming of the railways the South Cave Market died out in the 1850s the Fair continued into the twentieth century attracting people from a wide area. An analysis of the 1841 Census

The Church of All Saints stands in the oldest part of South Cave. It was restored in 1601 and there was further rebuilding in the 19th century paid for by the Barnard family.

returns show some three hundred visitors arriving for the festivities and staying with friends and relatives in South Cave with a further eight hundred in surrounding villages. The importance of 'Cave Fair' to the local economy of the time can be seen by reference to the school logbooks of nearby North Newbald whose schoolmaster wrote on the 23rd May 1870:

> "Many pupils still absent employed in making preparations for Cave Fair"

In South Cave itself the fair was an eagerly awaited event with local people whitewashing or colour washing their houses, wearing their finest clothes and making the traditional cheesecakes that were so much part of the celebrations. A sarcastic Robert Sharp wrote in his diary on 25th May 1834:

"This is Cave Fair Sunday when there is no want of Hull gentry coming to stuff themselves with cheesecakes and who are particular not to forget their Cave friends at this time."

The first day of the Fair was traditionally associated with the sale of animals while the other days saw numerous 'pleasure' activities like plays, 'ass races' and 'wheelbarrow races' with South Cave's numerous hostelries eager to meet the needs of thirsty visitors and villagers. One of the most important was the 'Fox and Coney' a coaching inn dating back to 1739 with, in the early nineteenth century, stagecoaches stopping on the route between Hull and Thorne to provide weary travellers with refreshments.

Although the coming of the railways brought an end to the coaching trade the economy of 19th century South Cave continued to rely on farming and other rural occupations and a directory of 1892 lists twenty-seven farmers and thirteen market gardeners. Another aspect of stability was the continuing influence and patronage of the Barnard Family at Cave Castle with the education of village children benefiting from their generosity. In 1841 Mrs Barnard established a girls' school in the village and three years later the first part of a new school building was erected for them in Church Lane. A new boys' school was also built at a cost of £600 and opened in March 1895.

Since both schools also benefited from public funds they were subject to the usual checks by national and local inspectors. Reports held by the East Riding Archive Service are particularly revealing about the state of education in the village in the 1920s and 1930s. In general, Mrs Barnard's Girls' School seems to have been more successful than the Cross Church Boys' School. During a visit to the girls' school in November 1938, for example, the inspector reported:

"I find evidence of very thorough teaching. The Headmistress is very attentive to the preparation of her lessons and in consequence oral teaching is above average."

In comparison the inspector's reports on the boys' school, while making allowances for poor quality accommodation and playgrounds, were far more critical. After a visit on the 6th October 1937 the local inspector wrote:

26

At South Cave Carnival, 1911. (East Riding of Yorkshire Council, Library and Information Services)

> "The Headmaster is rather peculiar: very conscientious and knowledgeable but not very successful. When teaching he seems tired and worn out and dwells on unimportant details."

The differences between the two schools were stark with the inspector commenting on "evidence of splendid training in good habits" among the girls while the boys "do not seem to enjoy their lessons and they make little real effort."

Since the Second World War education in South Cave has undergone a remarkable transformation with a rise in pupil numbers, changes in the curriculum offered and considerable improvements in the quality of teaching. In the 1920s combined pupil numbers for South Cave's two elementary schools were about one hundred and thirty while in 2001 there were four hundred and forty pupils at South Cave Church of England Primary School which opened in 1967. This rise in numbers reflects the growing population of South Cave in the last fifty years with large numbers of new houses being built, for example Barnards Drive and Castle Rise.

Business activity too has seen huge changes in recent times with Cave Castle being transformed from a Victorian stately home to one of

Mrs Barnard's Girls School in Church Lane at South Cave. The first part of the building was erected in 1844 with other work being completed in 1866. It is now a private residence.

the areas leading hotels, complete with a health club and an eighteen-hole golf course with over three hundred and fifty members.

Another aspect of South Cave's growing reputation in the hospitality industry is the 'Fox and Coney Inn' at the heart of the Market Place Conservation Area. This award winning business combines the facilities of a hotel, with twelve en-suite rooms, a restaurant and a public house.

Meanwhile at the southern-end of the village another success story has been Waudby's Caravan Centre. Now over thirty years old the business had very humble origins as Howard Waudby explained:

> "Before 1975 the family ran a pig farming business. My father, Don Waudby, enjoyed caravan holidays but had a caravan that was too small for his needs and so he sold it. From that one sale he went on to sell other caravans and the business began to grow."

In the last sixty years therefore South Cave has developed far beyond the rural market village it once was. Now with the dimensions of a small town and a population of over 4,500, it has managed to retain the character and rural charm of yesteryear.

CHAPTER 5

TICKTON

In the twenty-first century building steel and concrete bridges across rivers is a commonplace achievement of modern civil engineering. Today, between the Humber and Tickton, over a dozen bridges span the River Hull with the Ennerdale Bridges at Kingswood providing a good example of the art of modern-day bridge building. However two hundred years ago the River Hull was a more formidable obstacle to communications since there were only two bridges across this well used waterway (North Bridge, Hull and Hull Bridge, Tickton). The second of these, commanding the important route from Beverley into Holderness, had existed since at least the thirteenth century for in the year 1264 it was recorded that rebels had broken down the wooden bridge there to prevent the barons and troops of Henry III from using it.

By the beginning of the nineteenth century the township of Tickton-cum-Hull Bridge had a stone bridge although the severity of its arch (to allow for river vessels to pass more easily underneath) sometimes caused problems for road users. In February 1869 we learn of an accident at the bridge as a horse and cart from Leven, building up speed to reach the top of the incline, came to grief!

In 1912 it was decided to replace the bridge with a more modern, opening, structure and Sir John Wolfe Barry and Partners of Westminster were successful with their tender of £9,140. This hydraulic bridge, with a span that could be rolled back to the Beverley side, was in turn replaced by a modern structure two hundred metres upstream when the Tickton by-pass was opened in 1974.

With both river and road transport available the area around the bridge was ideal for industrial development and this took place from the mid-eighteenth century. By 1823 a trade directory indicates that there was a malting business there while later in the century the Stephenson family of Beverley established a successful mill for crushing animal bones and linseed and for the manufacture of fertilisers and animal foodstuffs. By 1901 census records reveal the existence of a thriving industrial hamlet at Hull Bridge with a workforce of oil millers living in cottages close-by. Supervising operations at the mill was manager Arthur Stephenson who lived at Hull Bridge House with his wife Norah and two servants. Across the road from their home George Tomlinson, licensed victualler and

The old Tickton bridge on a winter's day around 1900. To the right are the wharf, mill and warehouses of Robert Stephenson and Co. (Image courtesy of the East Riding Museums Service)

cowkeeper, ran the 'Crown and Anchor' Public House serving refreshments to the crews of river vessels, industrial workers and thirsty travellers alike. This too was owned by the Stephenson family and a press cutting of December 1919, held by the East Riding Archive, shows the sale, at auction, of this famous Tickton inn to the Hull Brewery Company for £1800 10s 0d (£1800.50).

The Stephenson family, as befitting their wealth and importance in the community, proved to be important benefactors for Tickton's church whch was built in 1844 and its school which opened in 1848. Members of the family donated stained glass windows, a lectern and an organ to the church while in 1897 a bazaar held at the Stephenson's home helped to raise funds for a church restoration. A Christmas party for the children of the village was also a regular event at Hull Bridge House. In 1872 another of the Stephensons donated five almshouses to the village providing rent-free accommodation for some of Tickton's elderly poor.

Although the mill and warehouses of Robert Stephenson and Son fronting the River Hull have now disappeared being demolished in 1984, industry and commerce continues to thrive at Hull Bridge with a diverse range of businesses. One of these is 'Crème d'Or', a company that imports and distributes high quality European chocolate and confectionery.

The process of change is also evident elsewhere in the village. In 1823 the writer Edward Baines recorded that Tickton had a population of only a hundred and ten people. The village was then a small compact place on each side of the old main road in the area of Carr Lane. After 1850 the village began to expand eastwards with the building of more houses into 'New Tickton' so that by 1891 the population was three hundred and five. A local directory shows the usual trades of an East Riding village of the time including a shoemaker, a blacksmith and a bricklayer. By then the village had three public houses: the 'Crown and Anchor', the 'Board Inn' which closed around 1905 and the 'New Inn' which was built by 1861.

The County Inspector visited the Church School on Main Street Tickton regularly between 1921 and 1941 and his reports make interesting reading about both the strengths and weaknesses of those who taught there. In May 1921 there were seventy-five children on roll and the inspector wrote of its aging Head-Teacher :

"Miss Knox means very well and there is ample evidence of assiduous work but the bulk of it is on obsolete lines."

The old stone bridge being demolished c. 1913. A temporary bridge was constructed to the left of it. The new permanent Tickton Bridge (with a movable span to allow for the movement of river vessels) was later built on the site of the stone bridge. (Image courtesy of the East Riding Museums Service)

By March 1926 Mr Agerskow was in charge of the school and the inspector reported favourably on the improvements he had brought about. School inspection reports of that time frequently commented on the personalities of teachers and Tickton was no exception. In September 1930 the inspector wrote:

> "The headmaster is very enthusiastic and vigorous. He is perhaps a little too boisterous and excitable in manner and this causes him to appear somewhat rough and tactless."

Seven years later the inspector observed that Agerskow's pupils were following his example when he wrote:

> "I notice that the children of the school are rather noisy and restive like the Headmaster."

The Georgian elegance of the Tickton Grange Hotel.

The most dramatic changes in the village have happened since the Second World War and especially with the opening of the Tickton by-pass. This not only took traffic away from the main street but also released land for new house building so that by 1981 the village had eight hundred and seventy four residents. There have been impressive developments too with the village's two country mansions: 'Tickton Grange' and 'Tickton Hall'. 'Tickton Grange' at the eastern end of the village dates back to the 18th century and in a local directory of 1823 was called 'Mount Pleasant'. Its most notable owners were the Harrison-Broadley family who lived there from the late nineteenth century until the 1960s and one of them added a new east-wing to the building in 1926-1927. In 1979 this elegant Georgian mansion was bought by Peter and Sheila Whymant and became the 'Tickton Grange Hotel', one of East Yorkshire's most prestigious venues for conferences and weddings as well as for the quality accommodation it offers.

At the other end of the village stands 'Tickton Hall' bought in 1997 by local businessman and self-made millionaire Andrew Foreman. It is now the home of Beverley Polo Club and has some of the most lavish

Performers of the Tickton Little Theatre. (Image courtesy of the Tickton Little Theatre)

facilities in the UK including three outdoor grounds, an impressive indoor 50,000 square foot floodlit arena and stabling for up to sixty horses.

For those interested in the arts the village also has a great deal to offer. Far-sighted folk back in 1948 wanted a village hall and through voluntary effort were able to see this valuable community resource take shape. These days the hall is home to a number of activities including a bowls club, pre-school education and perhaps most impressive all the 'Tickton Little Theatre'.

As well as their own amateur annual pantomimes involving fifty local people or more the Little Theatre is actively involved in bringing professional theatre groups to the village hall. Working closely with the Hull Truck Theatre Company and supported by East Riding of Yorkshire Council Arts local residents are able to see productions like 'The Dying of the Light' and 'Bouncers'.

In the last fifty years therefore Tickton has grown far beyond the tiny rural community it once was. With a population now of over a thousand people the village continues to attract newcomers with its easy access to both Hull and Beverley.

CHAPTER 6

HUTTON CRANSWICK

Situated to the east of the A164 Beverley to Driffield road the villages of Hutton and Cranswick have now effectively merged into one although both have quite distinct characters. The name Hutton is thought to be derived from the Norse word 'hoot' or hill while the word Cranswick possibly came from 'cranes', birds which lived in the wetlands east of the village. The village of Cranswick was always the bigger of the two for it had a more plentiful supply of water although it was Hutton, standing on higher ground, that had the church. The Church of St Peter was built in Norman times replacing a Saxon church mentioned in the Domesday Book of 1086. In the late nineteenth century the building was extensively restored at a cost of three thousand pounds.

One of the major attractions of Cranswick is its extensive village green covering six and a half acres and claimed to be the largest in the East Riding. These days the green with its mature trees and village pond is a major visitor attraction and the area's numerous footpaths make the village a magnet for walkers. In the past the green was used to graze animals for both Hutton and Cranswick were essentially agrarian communities and a directory of 1823 lists seventeen farmers. Evidence of that past can be seen at Hutton where the tower of the village windmill still stands and where, in 1823, Thomas Dawson worked as the miller.

The prosperity and picturesque tranquillity of the Hutton Cranswick of today however is in marked contrast to the rural poverty experienced by some residents over a century ago. A local newspaper of July 19th 1879 recorded an inquest into the death of Martha Wilson, aged five, at a cottage midway between Hutton and Cranswick. Henry Wilson, farm labourer his wife and six children lived there in squalid conditions, sharing a single bedroom and vulnerable to any infectious disease. On the 3rd July one of the children caught diptheria and with the parents unable to afford medical help the child died three days later. However in their overcrowded hovel this highly contagious illness had been transmitted to Martha Wilson too. She also died and at her inquest Dr Wood, the medical officer for the district, gave his opinion that the house "was totally unfit for so many to live in and that it should be thoroughly disinfected and every precaution taken to prevent a spread of the disease."

The village green at Cranswick today with its attractive pond.

Hutton Cranswick Railway station around 1900.

In the days before the Welfare State extreme poverty was an ever-present risk especially if a family's breadwinner became too ill to work, died or simply chose to abandon his responsibilities. The authorities took a dim view of the latter since under the poor law families would then have to be supported by the parish. In March 1867 James Geall of Hutton Cranswick appeared before local magistrates charged with abandoning his wife and five children and allowing them to become a burden on the poor rates. He had been living in Hull for five months and his claims that his intention had been that of getting a house and sending for them was not believed by the magistrates who sentenced him to a month in prison.

Yet in other ways the lives of even the poorest inhabitants was perhaps better by the end of the nineteenth century than it had been earlier. The railway arrived in the village in October 1846 with the opening of the Hull to Bridlington line reducing the cost of commodities like coal and helping to stimulate employment both directly and through its effects on farming. However Hutton Cranswick Station and the line nearby was the scene of several accidents in the late nineteenth century due to poor safety procedures. In August 1872 an inquest was held into

Cranswick village green around 1900.

the death of a boy called John Lovel who had been knocked down and killed by a train on the level crossing near the station. From the evidence given at the inquest it is clear that the gatekeeper, Esther Dowson, was in the habit of letting her young daughter operate the gates for her. The jury returned a verdict of "accidental death" but recommended that a man should operate the crossing in future.

To assist children from poor families the passing of the 1870 Education Act gave a boost to schooling in Hutton Cranswick. In 1874 a 'Board School' for two hundred and sixty junior children was built near the village green at a cost of £850. There was also a separate infants school for one hundred and twenty pupils close by and this was the system inherited by East Riding County Council in 1902 when it took over responsibility for education from the local school board.

During the 1920s the two schools, which provided an education up to the age of fourteen, were visited by the County Council Inspector. His reports, held by the East Riding Archive Service give a fascinating account of education in Hutton Cranswick in the inter-war years and also of the animosity between Mrs Robinson, the headmistress of the infants' school and Mr Atkinson, the headmaster of the junior school in the early 1920s. In March 1922 the inspector wrote of their quarrel:

Hutton Cranswick Primary School.

"Mrs Robinson is the sort of woman who must be keeping everybody right and allows her keen sense of right and wrong to outrun her discretion. Probably with the very best of motherly intentions she has mixed herself up in his domestic affairs. This has been resented and I rather fear that Mrs Robinson's fighting spirit has caused her to get her own back by commenting on Mr Atkinson's conduct."

The ill feeling between the two of them was clearly of concern to the inspector who believed that the age of the headmistress, who was sixty-three, allowed a way out of the impasse through her retirement. He wrote in March 1923:

"Although she is still an effective Headmistress it would be well for the sake of peace to help her resign. She is still very bitter with regard to him and it looks as if their differences are of such a nature as not to be easily adjusted."

In the event, her departure allowed for the amalgamation of the two schools although the inspector's critical comments on the headmaster of the combined institution continued as before. There was implied censure of his old-fashioned teaching methods when the inspector wrote in July 1925:

"Twenty years ago this school might have been described as very satisfactory."

Yet, the inspector's views, it seems, had little effect for eight years later he wrote:

"Of its kind the work is very good but teaching is not on modern lines and the children have little training in finding things out for themselves"

The kind of dull, mechanical learning by rote clearly in evidence in the 1920s and 1930s is in marked contrast to the kind of education provided at today's Hutton Cranswick Primary School for in 2005 an OFSTED inspection reported that lessons:

"successfully capture the interest of pupils through carefully planned stimulating activities."

Just as education in the village has changed to meet the rising expectations of pupils and parents so too has the economy of this thriving community. Back in the 1960s Hutton Cranswick still had seventeen working farms but the changing fortunes of agriculture in a global economy have helped to stimulate new businesses. Many of these are centred on Hutton Cranswick's old airfield. This had opened in 1942 as a fighter base and was part of Yorkshire's contribution to the air war against Nazi Germany. One of the most significant businesses located there has been Cranswick Mill. The operation began in 1974 when a group of farmers joined together to manufacture pig feed. From these beginnings Cranswick developed into a public company and diversified into many aspects of food production, including pork products like ham and sausages, at several sites in the United Kingdom. By 2007 Cranswick PLC was employing over four and a half thousand people and was generating sales of five hundred and twenty five million pounds a year.

The old windmill at Hutton around 1905.

When the journalist Edward Baines visited Hutton Cranswick in the year 1823 he recorded that the parish had a population of just nine hundred and seventeen people. In the twenty-first century that population has grown to over two thousand eight hundred. With easy car access to Driffield and Beverley and a conveniently located railway station Hutton Cranswick has become a popular commuter village.

CHAPTER 7

HOLME-UPON-SPALDING MOOR

When approaching Holme on Spalding Moor along the A164 road the first thing any visitor notices is the high hill that dominates the surrounding, flat, countryside. Known as Beacon Hill this prominent local landmark is the site of All Saints Church dating from the thirteenth century and serving the spiritual needs of the villagers living beneath. The high location of the church is understandable when you consider that the word Holme is derived from the Danish word for island. For much of its history the place would have been just that: an island isolated by the extensive marshes of Spalding Moor. The journalist Edward Baines, writing in 1823, reported that:

> "There are persons yet living who can remember the time when in foggy weather it was considered dangerous to cross them without a guide."

In such a desolate place as this another danger was highway robbery. One of these robbers was Snowdon Dunhill who was born locally in around 1760. He and his gang robbed unwary travellers on the roads across the marsh but was caught and transported to Botany Bay for his crimes.

Although the name Holme comes from the Danish settlers who arrived here from the ninth century the place is in fact much older. Excavations at Hasholme in the south-east of the parish in 1984 revealed the existence of an iron-age logboat, twelve and a half metres long dating from around 450 BC. The remains of the boat can be admired at the Hull and East Riding Museum.

Like most East Riding villages until recent times Holme on Spalding Moor was essentially a farming community and the enclosure of the lands around the village in 1773 began the process of change that saw the draining of the Spalding marshes and their replacement by the neat 'patchwork quilt' of fields of today. A directory of 1823 listed thirteen farmers/yeomen and their farms would have supported many more landless labourers living in the village or close by. Edward Baines was impressed by the fact that some of the main landowners of the area had allocated grazing land to this class of labouring poor and that this had

The Church of All-Saints stands on Beacon Hill about half a mile east of the village.

The former workhouse of Holme and Spalding Moor (built around 1790) - now Workhouse Farm. Originally there were two lock-ups at the workhouse (one for men, one for women) to punish those who broke the rules. The western lock up survives helped by restoration work in 1975. The structure is now a listed building.

"materially tended to the comfort of their families and to the ease of the parish."

In the early nineteenth century the parish was responsible for the various classes of paupers to be found in any community like Holme on Spalding Moor - for example orphans too young to work, the infirm and the elderly poor. A poor rate was levied on those wealthy enough to pay, mainly the landowners and tenant farmers, and the money raised was used to provide allowances to paupers living in their own homes and to build a workhouse for the homeless poor of the parish.

The workhouse for Holme was built on the Howden Road around 1790 and the buildings still stand at Workhouse Farm. There were separate quarters for men and women together with a governor's house and two small circular "lock-ups" where those who had broken the workhouse rules or had committed petty offences would be confined as a punishment. One of the village paupers who may have suffered this fate was Isabella White. On the 8th January 1816 she was brought before an East Riding magistrate charged with running away from the workhouse and taking with her a gown and two pairs of stockings "the property of the overseers of the poor of the said parish." Some of the other inmates could be equally troublesome. Records in the East Riding Archive dated the 19th June 1833, record how another pauper, Thomas Rosindale, had absconded for three days and then on his return had "conducted himself in a disorderly and riotous manner" towards the governor of the workhouse, William Clark.

Of course, the parish authorities were only responsible for their own poor and outsiders who 'wandered abroad collecting alms under false pretences' often fell foul of the vagrancy laws. In the 1820's and 1830's during a time of high food prices and unemployment a large number of these desperate people were arrested in the village and prosecuted as vagrants. Among them were John Turner and his wife Jane, who were convicted in November 1829 of begging and sentenced to a month in the Beverley House of Correction with hard labour and Isaac Robertson, Irishman, his wife Hannah and two children who were convicted in April 1830 of begging and sentenced to three weeks in the House of Correction.

Despite these examples of poverty it would be easy to exaggerate the hardships of life in the village in the nineteenth century. From the evidence of local directories it seems that Holme on Spalding Moor had a bustling economy and a directory of 1857 lists a number of trades including three tailors, four shoemakers, four blacksmiths and seven

Chauffeur driven cars outside the Blacksmith's Arms around 1900.

shopkeepers. All these trades were needed to support a population that had grown, by 1881, to one thousand eight hundred and ninety eight people.

Some of the names that appeared in nineteenth century directories of the village are still there today including the Blacksmith's Arms Public House and A. Laverack and Son, Family Butchers. The name Laverack has been a feature of Home on Spalding Moor for at least one hundred and fifty years for the 1857 directory of the village included a Jewitt Laverack, butcher and farmer. These days a fifth generation member of the family Tim Laverack and his wife Dawn, run both the village butcher's shop and the village bakery and the business has grown to include premises behind their shop at 50 High Street manufacturing a range of savoury items like pies and sausages.

'The Blacksmith's Arms' was built around 1822 and the directory of the following year records that John Hudson combined his work as a blacksmith with being a publican. It was once a coaching inn on the routes to Selby and Scarborough. However the arrival of the railway at Holme from 1848 (the Selby to Market Weighton line) would have brought a swift end to this trade.

The eastern end of the main street of Holme on Spalding Moor.

Perhaps the greatest village success story of years gone by was its role in establishing one of East Yorkshire's most prestigious companies: Northern Foods. In 1937 the Hull businessman Alec Horsley (1902-1993) opened a milk condensing plant in the village and from these small beginnings began the famous Northern Dairies and the multi-national company of Northern Foods. Today this enterprise, with its headquarters in Leeds, employs twenty-two thousand people and has annual sales of 1.4 billion pounds.

A mile south of the village centre other new businesses have been established at the former RAF airfield on Spalding Moor. This had begun life as a Bomber Command airfield in 1941 with three concrete runways. The first operational flight from the airfield took place on the night of October 21st 1941 when ten Wellington bombers attacked Antwerp in Nazi–occupied Belgium. One aircraft was lost during the operation when it came under attack from a German ME 110 fighter. There was only one survivor who spent the rest of the war in a POW camp. During its wartime role one hundred and fifty one aircraft operating from Holme

Holme-upon-Spalding Moor from Beacon Hill.

were lost and a memorial to those who gave their lives still stands at the entrance to the former airfield.

In the early nineteenth century Holme-upon-Spalding Moor was described as a 'large and scattered' village and remains so even today. In the 2001 census Holme on Spalding Moor parish had a population of 2,948 and the popularity of the village has meant that a considerable number of new houses have been built there.

CHAPTER 8

BROUGH

For many years the thriving East Yorkshire community of Brough has effectively been joined to nearby Elloughton by modern housing development. Two hundred years ago however Brough was a distinct village in its own right, surrounded by open countryside and with a tiny population of just 124 people. Historically its strategic position at the junction of Brough Haven and the River Humber meant that this ancient settlement had an importance dating back to Roman times.

"What did the Romans ever do for us?" was a question famously posed in the Monty Python film 'The Life of Brian'. In fact the same question could once have been asked by the inhabitants of Brough since many of them, in the 19th century, suspected that their village was the site of the Roman settlement of Petuaria but had little else to go on except occasional finds of Roman coins and pottery. Antiquarians too believed that Brough was the location of Roman Petuaria since it lay on the route of Roman roads linking Lincoln and York.

The Roman conquest of Britain had begun in AD 43 when Emperor Claudius sent an army under the command of Aulus Plautius. In AD71 prompted by a rebellion of one of the tribes of northern Britain, the Brigantes, the Romans crossed the River Humber (or the Abus Fluvius as it was known to them) and began the incorporation of East Yorkshire and other areas of northern Britain into their Empire. The East Riding was already inhabited by the Celtic people known as the Parisi tribe and, unlike the Brigantes, it seems that that these were peaceful and did not give the Romans trouble.

Although it had long been suspected that Brough was the site of a Roman fort and naval base, with the Haven providing a sheltered anchorage for shipping, a Quay for loading and unloading cargo and a ferry to link it with Winteringham on the south bank of the river, it was not until the 1930s that real proof was provided. An archaeological investigation of the area of the Burrs Playing Field, to the depth of about five feet, uncovered the foundations of Roman buildings. Another exciting find came separately in 1937 with an inscription on a stone slab. This recorded that a Roman magistrate, Marcus Ulpius Januarius, had from his own funds donated a new stage for Petuaria's theatre. The

Reconstruction of Roman Petuaria in the Hull and East Riding Museum, High Street, Hull. (Image courtesy of the Hull Museums Service)

inscription was in honour of the Emperor Antoninus Pius (AD138-161) and records the civic status of Petuaria as a vicus.

These and other finds in the early 1960's, like the discovery of shop foundations in a back garden at Grassdale Park, Brough, seem to suggest that by the second century AD Petuaria was more than just a military base to defend the river crossing and had taken on some of the trappings of Roman civilisation. The archaeological evidence also shows that by 270 AD the Roman settlement of Petuaria had grown to 12 acres in size and was surrounded by a 9ft thick stone wall.

The decline of Petuaria seems to have begun around the mid 4th century although when exactly it was abandoned is not known. Today nothing remains above ground to show us of its existence although anyone wishing to get a flavour of how Petuaria would have looked can visit the Museums Quarter in Hull's High Street to see the impressive reconstruction there.

Despite the fact that Roman Petuaria no longer exists, the name lives on in Brough itself. In August 2006 Brough's new £1.6 million Petuaria Centre opened on Centurion Way combining the functions of library, customer service centre and community facility. Another modern-day association with the name is the drama group called the Petuaria Players formed in 1960 and putting on three productions each year. The Petuaria Players celebrated its 100th play in 1996 with the J.B. Priestley period comedy 'When We Are Married.'

One of the underlying themes in the growth of Brough, since the 19th century, has been improved transport. It is clear that the importance of the place as a ferry crossing point on the Humber did not end with the departure of the Romans for Brough Ferry was often mentioned in the Middle Ages. An early 19th century history of the village records that:

> "The ferry at Brough is still much used for the conveyance of passengers, horses, etc to and from Winteringham"

At the heart of Old Brough is the 'Ferry Inn' dating back to 17th century where ferry passengers could obtain refreshments to fortify themselves for the occasionally stormy crossing. One of the Ferry Inn's links with the past concerns its associations with the notorious highwayman Dick Turpin. In 1738 Turpin had arrived in East Yorkshire masquerading as a gentleman called John Palmer after his criminal activities in the Home Counties had made it dangerous for him to remain there. One of the places he stayed at was the Ferry Inn at Brough and in

The traditional image of the highwayman Dick Turpin who in his guise of John Palmer had arrived at Brough in 1738.

his 'role' as Palmer and to finance his lifestyle as a country gentleman he made frequent excursions into Lincolnshire to commit more crimes. Documents held by the East Riding Archive in Beverley reveal his presence at the Ferry Inn. In a sworn statement to three East Riding justices, in October 1738, the publican, William Harris, claimed that Palmer had lodged with him for four or five months. Harris said that Palmer had made numerous trips into Lincolnshire returning with "several horses at a time" which he sold to "persons in the County of York." In his statement Harris claimed that 'Palmer' had told him that if he were to accompany him to Lincolnshire: "twenty pounds is as easily got as two pence."

It was Turpin's erratic, and probably drunken, antics at Brough, on the 2nd October 1738 that proved to be decisive in his capture. In a statement made on the same day as that of William Harris, two farm labourers, Abraham Green and John Robinson, claimed that Palmer had, without cause, shot dead "a tame fowl which did belong to Francis Hall of

Brough and did throw the said fowl into the fields of Elloughton." Furthermore, Robinson complained to the magistrates, that when he tried to remonstrate with Palmer about his unwarranted destruction of someone else's property, Palmer had threatened to shoot him too! The fact that these witness statements were made on the same day (October 3rd 1738) might suggest some degree of collaboration between Harris, Green and Robinson. Whether it was Harris who took the lead in bringing Palmer's activities to the notice of the authorities, and what his motive might have been, is unclear. However, Harris was the educated one of the three and in 1749 the record shows that he was paid to apprehend a Margaret Mitchil and her daughter Susannah and convey them to the Beverley House of Correction.

For the three East Riding magistrates meeting at Beverley on the 3rd October 1738 the evidence of Green, Robinson and Harris was enough for them to initiate further action. A warrant for the arrest of John Palmer was issued and he was arrested. It was only after his removal to York Castle that it was discovered that 'Palmer' was really 'Turpin' wanted in the Home Counties for robbery and murder. Dick Turpin was executed in front of a large crowd on York's Knavesmire on Saturday 7th April 1739.

Of great significance to the growth of Brough was the arrival of the railway on the 1st July 1840 when the Hull and Selby line opened. Coinciding with the opening of Brough Railway Station came the introduction of a steam ferry on the Brough crossing and the re-building of the 'Ferry Boat Inn' in 1841.

There is little doubt that the arrival of the railway made Brough a desirable place to live for those able to commute to work in Hull 10 miles away and the number of people in the village and in nearby Elloughton, began to grow as a result. By 1891 the population of Elloughton-cum-Brough was 927 an increase of 159% in just sixty years. A directory of the time described Brough as "a pleasant and thriving village" and its growing prosperity might be indicated by the existence of a ladies' school run by the Haldenby sisters and the "school for young gentlemen" of John Richardson.

If the arrival of the railway began the rapid growth of Brough then an acceleration of this process came in 1916 with a growing interest in the village by the Blackburn Aircraft Company. Robert Blackburn was a Leeds-based aeronautical pioneer whose business had been boosted by the outbreak of the First World War and by a government order for a hundred biplanes. He developed an interest in planes that could take off and land on water and in 1916 dispatched one of his staff, Mark Swann, to find a

Robert Blackburn was a Leeds-based aeronautical pioneer. In 1917 Brough was chosen as the site of a seaplane testing base by the Blackburn Aircraft Company and the aircraft factory subsequently developed from this decision. (Image courtesy of the British Aerospace Heritage Centre, Brough)

suitable base for a seaplane testing facility. Brough with its easy access to the Humber, its railway station and available land to build an aerodrome was the site Swann recommended.

It was soon to become far more than a place to test seaplanes for between 1928 and 1932 much of the work of the Blackburn Aircraft Company in Leeds was transferred there too. The re-armament years of the 1930s leading up to the Second World War led not only to the development of the factory but also of Brough itself with much housing development for the growing workforce. It was a trend that has continued since 1945 with the Brough factory producing famous aircraft like the Blackburn Beverley and the world-beating Buccaneer that first saw service with the Royal Navy in 1959 and dominated production at the factory for the next 19 years. Such was the aircraft's importance that the 'Railway Tavern' in Brough was re-named the 'Buccaneer' in 1962.

The opening of the Hull and Selby Railway in 1840 and with it Brough Station, helped to boost the population of the village.

These days the Brough factory of BAE systems is known as the 'Home of the Hawk', the jet trainer that is the mainstay of the 2,000 staff working at the plant.

In 2001 the total population of Elloughton-cum-Brough stood at over 7,000 people and ten years later it is higher still thanks to new housing developments on the south side of Welton Road where greenhouses once stood. Helped by good access to the M62 and A63 and a thriving rail service Brough has grown from a quiet 19th century village into a bustling urban area with a range of shops, banks and other businesses to cater for its ever expanding population.

CHAPTER 9

MIDDLETON-ON-THE-WOLDS

Like many East Riding villages that of Middleton-on-the-Wolds, situated in a valley about eight miles south-west of Driffield, seems to have had its origins in the Germanic invasions of eastern England from the fifth century. The name Middleton is derived from the Saxon words meaning 'middle farmstead' and there are many other examples of the same name being used elsewhere. Called Middeltun in the Domesday Book of 1086, the church of St Andrew, built on rising ground, dominates the eastern end of the village and dates back to the thirteenth century. Beneath it and around the junction of roads to North Dalton and Beverley this ancient Wold's community gradually developed. The village pond and wells would have ensured that there was a good supply of water in the days before this vital commodity came on tap. Near the pond a block of single-storey early eighteenth century chalkstone cottages, now forming a single house called 'Quackers', remain as an important reminder of Middleton's agrarian past.

In the centuries that followed the Norman Conquest farming remained the mainstay of the local economy with twenty-one farmers named in a directory of 1823. These trade directories generally listed only the most important people in the community such as farmers, tradesmen and shopkeepers and of the four hundred and forty one people in the parish in that year most would have been landless labourers and they and their dependents would have relied on others for employment. From records held by the East Riding Archive however we can sometimes get a glimpse of the lives of this social underclass. In a statement sworn before the local magistrate John Grimston on October 19th 1762, we learn of a complaint by Jane Dook, a servant in husbandry, against the Middleton farmer Richard Wiles. She complained that she had "been beaten, bruised and abused by her master without any just provocation or cause whatsoever."

While the law could sometimes protect this underclass from unfair treatment it could also be harsh towards those who neglected their duty or were found guilty of minor offences. In October 1828 the Middleton labourer Matthew Ircliff was charged with abandoning his wife and three children and leaving them dependent on parish relief. For this offence he

Early eighteenth century chalkstone cottages, now forming a single house called 'Quackers'.

was sentenced to three months imprisonment in the Beverley House of Correction.

One of the people named in the 1823 directory of the village was John Petch the licensee of the 'Robin Hood' public house but court proceedings of the same period also indicate his readiness to break the law. In August 1834 he was found guilty of allowing drunkenness on his premises on a Sunday and was fined two pounds plus costs. Newspaper reports from the nineteenth century indicate that alcohol was often a significant cause of disturbance in the village and like other parishes Middleton had its own set of stocks to punish those guilty of drunkenness or other minor crimes. The stocks were a punishment that confined the legs of petty criminals and exposed these lawbreakers to public ridicule. A village history of Middleton from 1892 recorded that the last use of the stocks in the village took place in June 1854 when a man was placed in them although the nature of his crime is unknown.

Although by the later nineteenth century the stocks were no longer in use to combat demon drink the courts continued to hear cases typical of any rural community of that time. One of the most notorious incidents was that of the publican Martin Lawlor, aged 63, who pleaded guilty to unlawful wounding at Middleton on the 12th May 1897. He had been charged with shooting Henry Simpson with a revolver occasioning actual bodily harm. Newspaper accounts of his trial suggest that Lawlor was intoxicated at the time.

Like many villages in the East Riding the population of Middleton continued to grow in the nineteenth century and by 1891 the parish had six hundred and seventy eight people living there. To cater for the needs of its children a Church of England School was built on Front Street in 1872 at a cost of £960. When the East Riding County Council Schools' Inspector visited Middleton in April 1921 he was unimpressed with both the school building and the children who he described as "rough, stodgy, untidy and uncouth." The inspector placed some of the blame for the school's failings on the headmaster who he claimed was 'out-of-touch' with modern teaching methods. In December 1921 the inspector wrote:

"A stronger man would I think do much to improve the manners and general behaviour of the children."

Throughout the 1920's these negative reports continued with the inspector commenting regularly on the "unattractive personality" of the Headmaster. In January 1925 the inspector wrote that the Head was "a

The Pond in the 1940s.

well meaning man, fairly conscientious but not nearly such a good headmaster as he is inclined to think."

It was probably with some relief, to the inspector at least, that this headmaster retired in 1934. However it is an indication of the problems of running a school at a time of tight budgets when he reported in October 1937 on 'extravagant spending' on textbooks. All the pupils in the top class had been provided with their own copy of 'Living Things for Lively Youngsters' at 3s 6d each (17p) and the inspector wrote disapprovingly:

"One copy for the teacher's use with the aid of a blackboard would have been just as effective"

The poor impressions of the Middleton Church School given by the inspection reports of the 1920s and 1930s are in marked contrast to the modern-day school in Station Road which was built 1967. In May 2008 an OFSTED inspection report declared that the personal development of pupils there was "outstanding", that their achievement was good and that standards were above average. A number of factors might explain the differences between the old school and the new including better resources, a well-trained more professional teaching force and the higher aspirations of parents and pupils. The Middleton-on-the Wolds of the inter-war years was a more insular place, despite the arrival of the railway in 1890, whereas since the Second World War the village has seen an influx of newcomers with the building of more houses such as those in Greenfield Road and Orchard Drive.

The village is situated on the busy A614 route between Market Weighton and Driffield and its shops and pub benefit from a lively passing trade. A major occasion that brings more people to the village each year is the famous Kiplingcotes Derby for the 'winning post' of the race is situated at the western end of the parish. It is reputed that the Kiplingcotes Derby began in 1519 during the reign of King Henry VIII and it probably originated as an event for the East Riding gentry to match their horses after the long winter months. The race had become important enough by the seventeenth century to become endowed with funds by leading figures of the day including Sir John Hotham and Sir Marmaduke Constable. These benefactors provided an investment fund that generated an income for prize money.

Spectators come from far and wide to watch the race and gather at the 'finishing post' since formalities such as weighing the riders and

The Kipplingcoates Derby takes place near Middleton each year in March. (Image courtesy of Jonathan Palmer)

reading out the rules also take place here before the race begins. One of these rules states that:

> "Every horse that runs for the prize shall start bridled and saddled and shall run with the rider weighing 10 stone."

Any rider under the weight limit can make up the shortfall by carrying weights in their clothes. In the year 2000, for example, the weight rule meant that Laura Crawford, who was the winner of the previous year's event, had to carry two stones of sand in her clothing. Other riders have been known to wear spanners, tyre levers and other tools to make up their weight to the required level. Neither can the riders afford to lose weight during the race; in 1961 one rider lost most of her lead weights from her pockets and weighed in 11lbs lighter than the required 10 stone. Even though she passed the winning post first the lady in question was disqualified.

After the formalities, the participants make their way to the start post in the parish of Etton four and a half miles away and when the race gets under way have to contend with a 'racecourse' consisting of farm

The Main Street at Middleton-on-the-Wolds.

lanes, grass verges and tracks. It is an indication of the strenuous nature of the challenge facing them that the starting post is 160 feet above sea level while the finishing post is 450 feet. Adding to their burden is the unpredictable March weather with cold biting winds, stinging rain and snow. Under these gruelling conditions the course can take its toll of the entrants and in 1966 and 1979 horses collapsed at the end of the race and died.

The glory involved in winning England's oldest horse race is far greater than any monetary reward for another peculiarity of the rules is that the winner has frequently received less prize money than the runner-up! This came about because the prize for being first was generated from the interest on the invested funds of the trustees while the prize for runner-up was derived from the entrance fee of £4.25. In the year 2000, for example, with eighteen riders taking part the entrance fees gave second-place rider Ken Holmes a prize of £72 while the winner, Fiona Nixon of Easington, only received £50 although she did receive the trophy. Another peculiarity of the race is that no one knows until the race day itself how many riders will turn up with their horses to take part. The numbers who compete vary widely from year to year and in the cruel winter of 1947 there was only one contestant. Fred Stephenson on 'Londesbrough Lad' struggled through snowdrifts four feet deep in order to complete the course and keep the race alive.

It is the quaint and seemingly incomprehensible features of the Kiplingcotes Derby which make the event such a well loved part of East Yorkshire's heritage and explain why riders and spectators loyally return to the parish of Middleton-on-the Wolds each year to witness the spectacle of England's oldest flat race.

CHAPTER 10

STAMFORD BRIDGE

Anyone travelling into the East Riding from York along the busy A166 road will have had cause to remember Stamford Bridge since the bridge itself is often the cause of bottlenecks with lights controlling the single lane of traffic. The bridge is a Grade 2 listed structure designed by William Etty of York who was paid the princely sum of £14 18s 0d (£14.90) for his work in 1723. The three-arch stone bridge was opened four years later and with occasional closures for maintenance work has been in constant use ever since.

River crossing points, either by ford or by bridge, were once of strategic importance and this explains the significance of Stamford Bridge in times gone by. The name 'Stamford' comes from the Angles, a Germanic tribe who settled in Eastern England from the fifth century, and means a 'stone-paved ford'. However before their arrival the Romans were here too; their settlement of 'Derventio' lay about one mile south of the present-day village and was on the important road to Eboracum (York) seven miles away.

By Norman times the settlement at Stamford Bridge had a wooden bridge and was known as Pons Belli (Battle Bridge) in celebration of the bloody encounter between the Saxons and the Norwegians that took place here on September 25th 1066. The Battle of Stamford Bridge was the result of events set in chain by the death of the English king Edward the Confessor on the 5th January 1066. His successor Harold Godwinsson, Earl of Wessex, was not of royal descent and there were other claimants prepared to resist his coup d'etat notably William, Duke of Normandy and Harald Hardrada, King of Norway.

Hardrada was a ruthless and murderous Norse warrior and was aided in his invasion plans by the English king's renegade brother, Earl Tostig. They defeated a Saxon army at the Battle of Fulford on the 20th September but to avoid any treachery in the aftermath a hostage exchange was arranged between the Saxons and the Norwegians for the 25th September 1066 at Stamford Bridge. In the event Hardrada and Tostig badly miscalculated the response of Harold Goowinnson to their invasion of Yorkshire. Perhaps they assumed that he would remain inactive in the south awaiting the invasion by Duke William from Normandy and thus give them time to consolidate their earlier success. However Harold's

A rather fanciful representation of the Battle of Stamford Bridge by the nineteenth century Norwegian artist Peter Arbo.

reaction to the news from the north was swift and decisive. By the 20th September, the same day as the Battle of Fulford, Harold's newly raised Saxon army began an epic journey north and covered the 185 miles from London to Yorkshire in just four days, gathering other troops along the way. By the night of the 24th to the 25th September they were in Tadcaster and the following day moved on to York where, it seemed, Harold learned of the rendezvous at Stamford Bridge.

From contemporary sources it would seem that King Harold's march on Stamford Bridge took the Norwegians and their allies by surprise for it was said that he "came upon them unawares beyond the bridge." According to local legend, supported by some historical sources, one heroic Norwegian single-handedly blocked the narrow wooden bridge over the Derwent preventing the Saxons from crossing it until he was killed by a spear thrust from underneath. Whatever the truth of this legend it would seem that Hardrada and his men were ill-prepared to meet the tide of Saxon housecarls and other troops who swept across the river and up the hill to meet them on Battle Flats. According to the Norse Sagas Hardrada died a heroic death by trying to rally his own men through personal courage but received "a wound in the front of his throat so that blood straightaway gushed from his mouth" and so died along with all those who stood near him. It seems that the battle went on until late in the day but that after Tostig too was killed it ended with a rout of the remaining Norsemen as they tried to flee back to their ships moored twelve miles away.

The Battle of Stamford Bridge thus ended in a Saxon victory and a huge though indeterminate loss of life, particularly so for the invaders. The writings of Orderic Vitalis (1075-1142) provided a macabre postscript to the battle itself when he recorded: "the field of battle may easily be discovered by travellers as great heaps of the bones of the slain lie there to this day, memorials of the prodigious numbers which fell on both sides."

Yet while King Harold had emerged triumphant his was to be a hollow victory since within days news was brought of Duke William's invasion from Normandy. By moving north to deal with Hardrada and Tostig, Harold was unable to oppose the Norman landing on the south coast. Furthermore the losses that the Saxons endured at Stamford Bridge forced Harold to confront William three weeks later with an army that was both weaker and more exhausted than it had been on the 20th September when it had set off north. On October 14th 1066 Harold was killed and the Saxons defeated at the Battle of Hastings. Yet, the outcome of the Norman invasion of England might have been very different if the Battle of Stamford Bridge had not taken place.

In the centuries that followed the battle, Stamford Bridge continued to grow thanks to its communications by both road and river. The Derwent was also used to power corn mills and fulling mills (for the manufacture of woollen cloth) from at least the 12th century. From documents held in the East Riding Archive we learn of a calamity that struck the corn mill at Stamford Bridge on October 20th 1749. From the evidence of its owner, George Wood, and others we know that around 8pm a fire began "which by the violence thereof in a short space of time" burnt the mill to the ground. A petition of that time asked for financial help for George Wood since the fire had left him "literally ruined and undone." The mill was subsequently rebuilt and in the nineteenth century £1000 was spent on it to extend it still further. By the time of its closure in 1964 there were two waterwheels and seven pairs of grinding stones and some the machinery was kept in place when the Corn Mill became a restaurant in 1967. Today this imposing Stamford Bridge landmark has been saved for future generations by turning it into apartments.

From evidence in the East Riding Archive it is clear that Stamford Bridge had become a fairly prosperous place by the late eighteenth century with some of its richer inhabitants eager to benefit from new business opportunities. Two of these were John Rotherford, a miller and William Cooper an innkeeper who entered into lucrative agreements with the local turnpike trust to collect the road tolls at Stamford Bridge Toll Bar. By 1813 they were paying £290 a year for this privilege whereas in 1788 the rent had been only £100.

Of course, not all of the village's inhabitants were as fortunate and some of Stamford's Bridge's poorest residents, such as widows or the elderly, looked to the parish for relief. The account books of the Overseers of the Poor provide details of payments financed by the ratepayers in support of paupers like Ann Boynton. One entry for November 23rd 1767 records: "Paid for coals and bedding for Ann Boynton- 4s 9d" (24p).

By the mid-nineteenth century Stamford Bridge was continuing to grow and according to a directory of 1855 the village enjoyed "considerable traffic on the Derwent." Yet, this river trade in coal, lime, corn and flour was increasingly curtailed by the arrival of the York to Market Weighton railway line in 1847. Stamford Bridge now had its own station and a magnificent fifteen arch brick viaduct with a central iron span to carry the track high over the Derwent. Although the line was

Stamford Bridge today. This eighteenth century bridge was designed by William Etty of York.

The main square of Stamford Bridge under water again in 2007.

closed in 1964 during the 'Beeching Cuts' the viaduct remains and for walkers visiting the area the old track bed of the railway provides an interesting route for them to follow.

In common with many other East Riding villages Stamford Bridge in the nineteenth century had a number of trades that today have vanished. Slater's Directory of 1855, for example, recorded the presence in the village of three shoe makers, two tailors, five grocers and three joiners /wheelwrights. Although these occupations have now gone a growing population supports other businesses including an electrical retailers called Rutherfords that evolved from a motor garage business of the 1930s.

At times of high rainfall the position of Stamford Bridge next to the River Derwent has placed it in the 'front line' in the battle against the ravages of Mother Nature. In early March 1999 4.9 inches of rain fell in the Derwent catchment area and by 7th March large parts of the village centre were flooded with people having to resort to canoes to move about. 'The Swordsman' Public House was particularly hard hit with the downstairs part of the pub waist deep in water. In November 2000 the floods returned when the Derwent burst its banks seriously affecting thirty businesses and homes and blocking the A166 road through the village. With Stamford Bridge having been flooded twice in two years the Yorkshire Flood Defence Committee now made the village a priority and a network of earth banks and floodwalls was built at a cost of £3.7 million. However, even these defences could not protect the village completely and the village square was once more under water on the 26th June 2007 during the disastrous floods that affected large parts of Hull and the East Riding.

Despite these problems Stamford Bridge has recovered well and continues to be a thriving community and a popular dormitory settlement for York. New house building in recent times has seen the population rise and in the 2001 census there were 3,394 people living in the parish making this community on the western fringe of the East Riding one of the most populous in the county.

CHAPTER 11

WARTER

In the last sixty years many villages in the East Riding have seen a rapid expansion as the growth of car ownership has allowed people to enjoy the benefits of country living but commute to work in major centres of population like York, Beverley and Hull. However some places have defied this trend and have smaller populations today than they did a century ago. One of these is Warter, sixteen miles east of York on the B1246 Pocklington to Driffield road and surrounded by the glorious countryside of the Yorkshire Wolds. In 1901 this pretty village had a population of 559 people but by 2001 this had shrunk to 159. This ancient community is also unusual in that it is an estate village where for the last three hundred years all the properties have been in the hands of a single owner.

The origins of Warter can be traced back to at least the 12th century when a Norman landowner, Geoffrey Fitz Pain granted property to establish an Augustinian monastery here. The present Church of St James stands on the site of the priory church while in the field to the north earthworks indicate where the other monastic buildings once stood. Warter Priory dominated life here for four hundred years (1132-1536) and the presence of this monastic house would have helped to stimulate the economy of the area. Like many East Riding villages, Warter soon had its own market and fairs but the turbulence of life in the Middle Ages is indicated when, in 1328, the fair was banned because of a number of murders that were committed there. Nor were the prior and canons of Warter Priory always above reproach themselves for reports and visitations from the 15th century indicate occasional wrongdoing. One prior, William York, was removed from office in 1457 by the archbishop after complaints of financial irregularities and his neglect of the monastery buildings.

With the dissolution of the monasteries during the reign of King Henry the Eighth came the closure of Warter Priory in 1536 and its property soon passed into private hands. However the name was to live on through the 'stately home' built about a mile from the village. This began life in the late 17th century as a relatively modest country residence built for the Pennington family who by the early 18th century owned virtually all the freehold property in the village. As Lords of the Manor their

The B1246 road runs through Warter which stands in a hollow of the Yorkshire Wolds.

Charles Wilson (1833-1907) bought the Warter Estate in 1878. He was a wealthy ship owner, a Liberal MP and was raised to the peerage as Lord Nunburnholme in 1906. (Image courtesy of the East Riding Museums Service)

influence on Warter cannot be overestimated for it was they who provided employment, rebuilt the church, built the school, began the improvement of village houses and set about enlarging Warter Priory itself.

Set amidst four hundred acres of parkland the occupants of the big house lived in rather grander style than the residents of the village whose lives they dominated. An official report of 1865 reveals just how bad conditions for ordinary Warter residents could be for it said:

> "Warter is an extraordinarily shabby village. The population has to put up with mouldy thatch, bulging walls, uneven floors,

73

Warter Priory from an old picture postcard. Warter Priory lay about a mile from the village and was surrounded by beautiful gardens and parkland. The house was begun in the late 17th century but additions by Charles Wilson after 1878 created a Victorian-Gothic country mansion. The house was demolished in 1972.

windows that will not open and doors that will not shut. They have to sleep in windowless and chimneyless lofts."

Perhaps stung into action by these adverse comments the Lord of the Manor, Lord Muncaster, soon began to build better houses for his tenants and this was a process continued by his successor, Charles Wilson, after he bought the 11,000 acre Warter Estate in 1878. Wilson was a wealthy ship owner from Hull and a director of the Hull Dock Company and the North Eastern Railway. His rise to prominence was marked by his selection as Sheriff of Hull in 1870 and his election as its Member of Parliament in 1870.

Charles Wilson was raised to the peerage in 1906 as Lord Nunburnholme but long before this he had begun to add to his mansion at Warter Priory in order to live in the style of a country gentleman. Resembling a French chateau with a new front, corner towers and ninety rooms here was a residence fit to entertain the cream of British society at events like formal dinners and weekend shooting parties. The 1891 census gives us some idea of the large numbers of domestic staff required to run such a large establishment. In addition to Charles Wilson, his wife, their six children and guests there were also twenty-three servants including butlers, footmen, cooks and housemaids.

Following the death of Lord Nunburnholme in October 1907 his wife continued to live at Warter Priory and to dominate the village and its inhabitants until 1929. This rather formidable lady controlled the village school through her agent and from inspection reports of the 1920s it is possible to glean something of the tensions that this situation created. A major issue was the state of the school building and on the 1st April 1921 the East Riding School Inspector wrote:

> "It is rather a pity that the building which is quite a good one is being allowed to fall into a state of disrepair"

A year later the inspector advised that "a tactfully worded letter might have the desired effect on the subject of repairs" but it seems clear that any complaints that the head teacher, Miss J Pollard, made fell on deaf ears for on the 21st March 1923 the inspector reported that repairs were "urgently needed since some of the window panes will fall out before long." The issue of the school buildings was one that was continue to occupy later head teachers too for the inspector was still commenting on the need for repairs to windows and woodwork in 1935.

It took a further forty years before the original school building (built in 1868) was replaced by modern premises. These days Warter Church of England Primary School has achieved an enviable reputation for the quality of education that it offers and in a 2005 report OFSTED said that many of its talented pupils "travel considerable distances to attend." However back in the 1920s and 1930s inspection reports were far less complimentary. In March 1930 the East Riding inspector made the astonishing claim that the head teacher was "inclined to look upon his pupils and the village as hopeless", that a large proportion of the pupils were "of poor native intelligence" and concluded that "the work of conducting this small school must be depressing."

In the 21st century the fortunes of Warter Primary School have been transformed and new buildings have replaced the old school. Other changes too are apparent. Like its predecessor the newer Warter Priory, described by some as a Victorian monstrosity, has now vanished: it was demolished after the last of its contents were auctioned in May 1972.

Another building that almost met the same fate was St James Church in the village. This had become redundant by the 1990s but was

Accomplished musician Troy Donockley is a resident of Warter and has a recording studio in the village. (Image courtesy of Troy Donockley)

rescued by the local community who formed a trust to buy it for one pound and helped to raise the £600,000 necessary to restore the Victorian building to its former glory. It is now the Yorkshire Heritage Centre but retains the best features of the period when it was used regularly as a church.

The Heritage and Arts Centre opened in September 2006 and is in regular use for events like family history days and art exhibitions as well as concerts. One of those who has performed there is Warter's own acclaimed musician Troy Donockley who has a recording studio in the village. Troy has built up a formidable international reputation as a virtuoso performer of the uilleann pipes and as a composer and arranger. His unique and highly acclaimed blend of English classical and Irish folk traditions has led to music from his albums 'The Unseen Stream' (1998) and 'The Pursuit of Illusion' (2003) being used by the BBC and Channel 4 for television programmes like 'Forgotten Britain' and 'Flamborough Head'.

Another of Warter's links with the arts is through the gifted Yorkshire artist David Hockney. In 2007 he produced his largest ever painting called 'Bigger Trees Near Warter'. This is a landscape composed

Manor Farm at Warter was re-built using brick in the early eighteenth century and was faced with dressed stone that was probably taken from the site of the Augustinian priory.

of fifty panels and measuring twelve metres long by five metres tall and was largely painted in the open air at a location close to the village during the winter months. The painting features a windbreak of beech trees together with a Wolds Cottage and was the biggest ever painting displayed at the Royal Academy in London during the summer of 2007. David Hockney has now donated this enormous work to the Tate Gallery immortalising the village of Warter for all time.

CHAPTER 12

KIRKELLA

One of the consequences of the popularity of suburban living is that places that were once distinct communities in their own right have been 'swallowed up' by the growth of modern housing. Kirkella is a case in point and as the green fields of yesteryear have disappeared under bricks and mortar the dividing lines separating it from other West Hull villages like Anlaby and Willerby have become blurred.

The growth of villages can sometimes be a fascinating business and through a study of old Ordnance Survey maps it is possible to investigate changes affecting localities over a period of time. A study of such maps, for example, reveals the links between the growth of Hull and the growth of Kirkella. With the outward expansion of Hull in the late eighteenth and nineteenth centuries came a desire of the 'well-to-do' to escape from the noise, smells and hustle of life in a growing commercial centre to a more peaceful and pleasant country environment. The village of Kirkella about five miles northwest of Hull was ideally placed to attract such settlement for as a house advertisement from 1771 said:

> "It is most desirably situated on a rising ground and commands an extensive and delightful prospect of the surrounding country, the town of Hull, the hills of Lincolnshire and the River Humber for an extent of thirty miles."

In fact the advantages of Kirkella as a place for settlement had long been recognised for it lay on a spring line between the higher land of the Yorkshire Wolds and the low-lying marshes and carrs leading down to the Humber. The place name 'Ella' and its alternative of 'Elverley' (used in the Middle Ages) suggests a history for the village dating back to Anglo-Saxon times and is thought to be derived from 'Aela's woodland clearing.' The prefix 'Kirk' indicates that there was a church here too and the Domesday Book of 1086, which suggests that around the time of the Norman Conquest there were only about thirty villagers, confirms this.

The Church of St Andrew, a part of which dates back to the thirteenth century, remains the oldest building in the village. Inside is an impressive monument in white marble to Joseph Sykes (1723-1805), a member of a rich Hull merchant family, and this provides evidence of

SCHOOL HOUSE. "SCOTT" SERIES. NO. 369.
KIRKELLA, NEAR HULL.

Kirkella Church of England Primary School was built 1859-1860 with funds and land given by Major Richard Sykes. There was a master's house incorporated into the school. In 1892 the schoolmaster was Henry Hurst.

St Andrews Church, Kirkella is a Grade 1 listed building. The chancel dates from the 13th century and the tower from the mid 15th century.

Kirk Ella House in Church Lane was built in 1779 and occupied by John Stephenson, a Hull merchant. After he died in 1786 it was sold to another Hull merchant, Thomas Howarth.

how Kirkella had became a desirable place to live by the beginning of the nineteenth century. Joseph Sykes had grown wealthy from his activities in the Swedish iron trade that supplied the Sheffield steel industry with its raw material. His wealth and social standing led him to be chosen as sheriff of Hull in 1754 and twice as mayor in 1761 and 1777 and from the 1750s he began buying land and property in Kirkella. His decision to move to a quieter and more wholesome location away from the noxious smells of Hull's High Street may have been influenced by the availability of better transport by road. In February 1745 the Hull-Anlaby-Kirkella Turnpike Trust was created by Act of Parliament and began to improve the condition of a road that hitherto had often been made impassable by flooding.

The purchase of West Ella Hall by Joseph Sykes in 1756 was an example soon followed by others from Hull's merchant elite. Close to the historic village centre is Kirkella House in Church Lane which was built in 1779 and owned, initially, by John Stephenson a Hull merchant and

Willerby and Kirkella Station opened in July 1885 and closed to passengers in August 1955.

subsequently by others of a similar social standing including the Hull banker Robert Pease.

By the time the journalist Edward Baines wrote about Kirkella in 1823 the population had risen to three hundred and sixty eight people and his village directory of that year listed fourteen people described as 'gentry' including Joseph Egginton (magistrate) and Anthony Jones (silversmith). Of course his directory also contained the names of those of more humble origins including a blacksmith, a butcher, two shopkeepers and two shoemakers.

Seventy years later a village directory of 1892 recorded a similar mix of gentlemen, professionals and tradesmen ranging from Daniel Sykes of Kirkella Hall to Miss Fanny Youngson, the licensee of the 'Wheatsheaf' Public House. Also listed in the directory was Robert Hellyer, a retired ship owner, living at Western Villa in the village. The 1881 census shows that Robert Hellyer, his wife Sarah and daughter Jane had been born at Brixham in Devon. It was the fishing trade that brought them to Hull for Robert Helyer was a trawler owner who grew rich on the profits of this rapidly expanding industry. He was thus able to fund his comfortable retirement years in the peaceful village of Kirkella. It is interesting to note however that when he died in 1912 his body was returned to Brixham for burial.

The 1892 directory also shows us that a number of villagers worked in Hull. These included Wilson Barkworth (solicitor) and James Gough a piano manufacturer of the firm Gough and Davy. These early commuters were able to make use of the nearby station on the Hull and Barnsley Railway which opened in July 1885, for a fast journey into work or a more sedate mode of transport using Samuel Binnington's horse-drawn bus that operated between Kirkella Church and Carr Lane in Hull. This was replaced by motor buses in 1914.

It was in fact the 'motor revolution' and a growing car ownership, more than any other factor, that helped to stimulate the growth of Kirkella in the 1920s and 1930s and which gathered pace in the decades after the Second World War. In the 1930s,for example, there was considerable new house building in places like Church Lane and Beverley Road, Kirkella. In the process some of the village's older properties with their extensive gardens, for example in Godman Lane, disappeared. One that has survived is Kirkella Hall in Packman Lane which was built around 1806-1810 and is now Hull Golf Club.

The Club had opened its first golf course on Hull's Anlaby Road in 1904 but had been given notice to quit in April 1923 after the City Council announced a road-widening scheme in the area. A letter of the 5[th]November 1923 told members of its proposed replacement by a course in Kirkella comprising:

> "Kirkella Hall with three cottages stables, gardens etc and parkland containing about forty eight acres and belonging to E. Starkey Wade, Esq together with an adjoining sixty acres of parkland belonging to Captain C.A.V. Sykes of West Ella."

The club paid Mr Wade the sum of £11,500 for Kirkella Hall, the cottages and the land and this included a seven-acre plot on Packman Lane not needed for the course and described as "eligible and ripe for building plots." The other land, which belonged to Mr Sykes, was at first leased and finally bought in 1945 for £12,117.The new course, designed by accomplished golf course designer James Braid, opened in May 1925 and has been in use ever since.

Kirkella's own golf course was yet another factor that enhanced the reputation of the village as a very desirable place to live and like

The former blacksmith's forge at the heart of 'Old Kirkella'.

Robert Helyer before many trawler skippers of the 1950s and 1960s aspired to have homes here. During a debate in the House of Commons in 1981 Kevin McNamara MP went as far as to claim "the foundations of the houses in Kirkella were built upon cod bones."

For other 'upwardly mobile' folk a Kirkella address also seemed to be essential and another good example was the singer David Whitfield (1926 to 1980). He was born in the dockland district of Drypool in Hull and when he left school at the age of fourteen went to work as a baker's delivery boy. However he also had ambitions to be a professional singer and his first engagement was at the Perth Street Club, Hull in 1942. The breakthrough came in 1950 when he appeared on a radio version of 'Opportunity Knocks' and his abilities as a singer brought him to the notice of the Decca Record Company who gave him a contract in 1954. He was soon an international star appearing on the Ed Sullivan Show in the USA a remarkable eight times and achieving a string of hits in the popular music charts of the time. Despite his worldwide success David Whitfield continued to maintain a presence locally and his newfound wealth enabled him to buy a house in Kirkella called 'Cara Mia'.

Internationally famous singing star David Whitfield lived at Kirkella in the 1960s.

The house was named after David Whitfield's most successful record of the 1950s. 'Cara Mia' was released in June 1954 and it stayed at the top of the British charts for a record ten weeks. The success of the song meant that he was the first UK male artist to earn a gold disc and the first British artist to get into the top ten of the US Billboard Top 100. Cara Mia sold a million copies in the United States alone.

Today Kirkella seems to be as popular a place to live as it was two hundred years ago when it became the favoured location of Hull's merchant class. In the 2001 census the parish had a population of 5,661 and other data points to a prosperity unsurpassed in East Yorkshire with the vast majority of households being owner-occupied.

CHAPTER 13

HUGGATE

One of the great joys of living in East Yorkshire is getting off the beaten track and exploring some of the less-well-known byways that cross the beautiful undulating landscape of the Yorkshire Wolds. One of these journeys takes you via Middleton-on-the-Wolds and North Dalton along minor roads to a point around 558 feet above sea-level and to the village of Huggate. The actual village lies in a hollow but even from a distance its beautiful parish church of St Mary with its distinctive spire dominates the surrounding area.

The name Huggate is thought to come from the Old Norse words 'haugr' and 'gata' (meaning a road near the mounds) for this was once a part of England controlled by Danish invaders of the ninth century. However the medieval church remains the oldest surviving building in the village. Parts of it date from the thirteenth century while the tower and spire were built in the fourteenth century and extensive restoration work took place in the nineteenth century. An interesting relic of former times in the church is a notice from the manor court of 1826 naming the twelve jurors who were entrusted with the task of controlling the way the land was farmed and who could impose fines for those who broke the rules. One of these rules stated that anyone allowing their geese to go into the streets should "forfeit one shilling for each offence."

Another of the rules of the Manor Court stated that every parish officer should present his accounts within twenty-one days of going out of office on pain of a fine of around two pounds "for each default". In a simple agrarian village like Huggate much depended on the work of unpaid officials chosen from the local community like the pinder who rounded up stray animals and the parish constable who arrested wrongdoers and brought them before local magistrates. Other parish officers were the overseers of the poor who levied a local rate or property tax on landowners for the support of paupers among the infirm, the elderly and unmarried mothers or made arrangements for the care of orphans.

After the passing of the Poor Law Amendment Act in 1834 Huggate became one of the forty-seven parishes and townships of the Pocklington Poor Law Union and gradually the use of the 'workhouse system' became the preferred way of dealing with paupers seeking help

The magnificent Church of St Mary with its distinctive steeple.
(Image courtesy of Stephen Horncastle)

from the parish. A new 'union workhouse' was built at Pocklington in 1852 at a cost of almost £2000 and by using census returns and other records it is possible to discover something about those who lived there. The 1871 Census for example reveals the presence at the Pocklington Workhouse of Jane Craven a former domestic servant who was born in Huggate. The parish registers of Huggate show that she was the daughter of William Craven an agricultural labourer and had been baptised at St Mary's Church in the village on July 23rd 1835. Although we know nothing of her early life the Pocklington workhouse 'admissions and discharge book' held by the East Riding Archive in Beverley shows that she had been admitted to the workhouse on the 8th March 1866 because she was "destitute."

Already the mother of three illegitimate children, who were also in the workhouse, Jane Craven was soon to be involved in a major scandal for on the 3rd April 1867 she made a statement to the Pocklington Poor Law Guardians to say:

"I am now with child and about seven months advanced. Mr Pattinson, the late master, is the father of it. The connexion took place about Martinmas last year. It was in my bedroom he came to me; the matron was out at the time. He had been in the town and had had some liquor. It occurred three or four times afterwards. The matron was at home the third time it occurred. It was in the kitchen about 10pm; the others had gone to bed. About two months after I told him I was in the family way. He wished me not to have it. He said he would give me something but did not."

William Pattinson was well aware that once the pregnancy was discovered his position as workhouse master and that of his wife as matron would be in jeopardy. He therefore persuaded Jane Craven to keep it a secret until he had made his plans to 'escape'. With an unblemished record he could expect the Guardians to provide testimonials to enable him and his wife to find new jobs elsewhere. Pattinson fully understood that if it became known that he was the father of Jane Craven's unborn child before these testimonials were secured then his future employment was seriously at risk.

From the statement given by Craven it is clear that Pattinson's wife was also part of the cover-up. She said:

The village pond around 1900 with water carts waiting to fill up.

"I told the matron just before she left. She said it was a very bad job but she could not help me."

Craven also suggested that Pattinson and his wife had neglected their duties at the workhouse by saying:

"They were often out until late and both together with only the schoolmaster left in the house".

To forestall any suggestions that her unborn child might have another father she declared:

"I have never been out of the house since I came into it. I am quite sure I have never had connexion with anyone else since I came to the house but the master W Pattinson."

Unable to sign her own name Jane Craven put her 'mark' on the statement and had it witnessed by others. The Pocklington Guardians then sent it with an explanatory letter to the Poor Law Board in London on the 6th April 1867 as proof of a conspiracy of silence. When asked about their opinion "as to the general character and conduct of Mr William Pattinson" the Guardians indicated that they had no reason to doubt him or his wife for they said:

"During his time they had been satisfied with the discharge of their duties. The workhouse had been kept clean, the books well kept and that the matron had been attentive to the sick."

Accordingly on their departure the couple had been given the appropriate testimonials by the Pocklington Guardians but discovered "shortly after" that Jane Craven was "with child".

Although by today's standards and those of the nineteenth century Pattinson had clearly acted in an unprofessional manner and had abused his position of trust the statement of Jane Craven does not indicate that there was any coercion on his part. The fact that the person writing the statement on Craven's behalf included the words: "I have three illegitimate children who are in the house" might imply that Jane Craven was no stranger to sexual encounters and indeed may have initiated the relationship with Pattinson.

Steam threshing at Huggate around 1909. (Image courtesy of the East Riding Museums Service)

While Jane Craven represented one of Huggate's poorer former residents at the other end of the social scale was George Clarkson who at the time of 1861 Census was described as "a farmer of six hundred and forty acres employing nine labourers and four boys." Three years earlier Clarkson had become a celebrity in the village when he was the intended victim of the 'Huggate Highwayman'.

In romantic fiction highwaymen are often portrayed as bold, gentlemanly, devil-may-care figures on horseback intercepting unwary travellers with the cry of "stand and deliver". In reality they were often vicious criminals quite prepared to use violence against their victims in order to rob them of anything of value. One of the most notorious was Dick Turpin who was executed in front of a large crowd on York's Knavesmire in April 1739.

The number of 'mounted robberies' had begun to decline by the late eighteenth century but the menace of 'highway robbery' was to continue to fascinate the public into the nineteenth century. Newspapers would often use the word 'highwayman' to describe those who were really 'footpads'; the 'Huggate Highwayman' was the name used by the 'Eastern Counties Herald' when describing an 'ambush' carried out by a criminal called James Ireland in January 1858.

On the night of the 14th January 1858 George Clarkson was returning on horseback from Driffield Market to his home at Huggate Lodge when he was:

> "savagely set upon by a highwayman who attempted to rob him within a mile of his own house."

Clarkson had however armed himself with a revolver because of the many burglaries and robberies in the neighbourhood and was able to fire five shots at his attacker.

Later in court Clarkson described what happened after his attacker had dragged him from his horse and assaulted him:

> "I was on the ground, wounded on the left side of my face. After a while he got the better of me and got me on my back. I kept hold of my revolver and fired it again twice as he was over me. He then made an effort to get to my breast pocket and I struck him with my pistol over the head and face and cried out 'murder' as loud as I could. I tried the fifth barrel but it misfired and he ran off with his clothes on fire."

Several clues were found near the crime scene including blood stains, a handkerchief, a bludgeon and some burnt pieces of cloth and using these and "information received" Driffield Police Superintendent Joseph Young set off on horseback in pursuit of the criminal. His journey took him via a lodging house eighteen miles away, to a surgeon in Scarborough where a man answering the description of the highwayman had sought medical help, to Whitby and finally to Guisborough. There, a week after the crime, Joseph Young "ran his man to earth in a lodging house." The suspect arrested was James Ireland a "powerfully built man" in his twenties whose "waistcoat was found to be burnt at the back with a bullet hole through the front of it."

The newspaper reported that there had already been several highway robberies in the Driffield area and that James Ireland, a powerful looking man in his twenties, was suspected of being one if not the foremost member of the gang responsible. When he appeared before Driffield magistrates in late January George Clarkson and others were there to give evidence. One of these was a surgeon who said that the prisoners "lower lip had been penetrated by a ball carrying away two of the fore teeth and part of the jaw. The lips were stained blue suggesting the effects of gunpowder."

Interestingly Clarkson was unable to identify the prisoner as the man who had attacked him since it was a dark night but it was the evidence of others especially the surgeon that convinced the magistrates that James Ireland had a case to answer. Another witness was Mary Barker from a lodging house at Burlington who said that she had seen the prisoner "bleeding profusely" from his face while another, Alice Stanton, identified the handkerchief found near Huggate as that belonging to James Ireland.

Ireland denied the charges and was then committed in January 1858 to stand trial at the York Assizes. With the typical speed of nineteenth century justice the case was heard in early March. The prisoner was charged with having "assaulted George Clarkson with intent to rob him". The Eastern Counties Herald in its edition of March 11th 1858 reported that Mr Thompson and Mr Cross appeared for the prosecution . However since he was a poor man at a time when there was no 'legal aid' James Ireland was undefended in court. George Clarkson again appeared to give evidence and said that despite firing his gun the man had got him off his horse and struck him a powerful blow on the head. After his attacker had run off with his clothes on fire Clarkson had then returned home and sent his servants back to the spot where the attack had happened. Here they had found a heavy bludgeon, a cap, a handkerchief and pieces of a blue shirt.

Having listened to the medical evidence about his facial wounds, about burnt clothing found at his lodgings and about a blue shirt he had been seen wearing the jury quickly found James Ireland guilty and he was sentenced to three years imprisonment. Despite the unfairness of a judicial system that denied him representation in court there seems little doubt of his guilt. However, it would be interesting to speculate about the fate of George Clarkson, the victim of the crime, in today's judicial 'climate' since he used a firearm to injure his attacker.

In the late nineteenth century Huggate was still very much a typical farming community and a directory of 1892 said of it:

> "The farms here are all in a high state of cultivation. Large numbers of sheep are reared in the valleys and on the hillsides."

This same directory named eight farmers and the village was also home to several tradesmen vital in such an isolated self-reliant

The Wolds Inn at Huggate is popular with visitors to the village.

community as this. These included two shopkeepers, a tailor, a shoemaker, a joiner/wheelwright and two blacksmiths. One of the blacksmiths was James Cooper and an account book from fifty years later in the East Riding Archive shows that this was very much a family business passed from generation to generation. By the late 1930s Thomas Cooper was in charge and an entry in his accounts dated July 5th 1938 shows that he charged three old pence (less than 2p in modern money) for sharpening a pair of hedge shears.

The trade directory of 1892 also includes the name of Henry Burton who was both a farmer and the licensee of the 'Wolds Inn'. This historic and famous public house is still in important part of the Huggate scene today. One part of the inn dates back to the sixteenth century and it still retains the cosy atmosphere of a traditional family-run pub with coal fires, wooden panelling and brassware. These days the 'Wolds Inn' is a popular venue for those who enjoy walking for the village lies on the Wolds Way and other footpaths. Walkers explore some of the hidden valleys of the Yorkshire Wolds that are only accessible on foot while in the village redundant farm buildings have been turned into luxury accommodation for them.

CHAPTER 14

COTTINGHAM

With claims to be England's largest village the ancient parish of Cottingham has a history dating back to the Bronze Age. Like other places close to Hull it saw considerable expansion from the eighteenth century as those of wealth and social standing moved here to enjoy the blessings of country living.

The name 'Cottingham' is thought to come from the time of the Anglo-Saxons in the fifth century and to mean the 'homestead of Cotta's people'. After the Norman Conquest of 1066 the manor of Cottingham was given to one of William's important henchman Robert Front de Boeuf and thence to the Stuteville family. By the thirteenth century it was the site of a 'castle' or fortified manor house. This stood on a mound and was protected by an inner moat and outer ditch and these features still exist. However the former site of 'Barnard Castle' is these days so surrounded by houses on Northgate and West End Road that it is only possible to catch brief glimpses of its ramparts. In the 14th century the original manor house fell into ruins but the name lived on through Cottingham's oldest secular building: a rarely seen 17th century half-timbered residence constructed within the confines of the 'castle' and reached by a private road off Hallgate.

Confusingly the village was also home to a second 'castle' although this was a nineteenth century creation of Hull banker Thomas Thompson. Around 1814 he created a manor house called 'Cottingham Castle' on a fifty-four acre site of rising ground to the west of the village but this was destroyed by fire in 1869. One reminder of this 'castle' that still exists is a 'turret' or folly built in the grounds of the original house. The estate was later bought by Hull Corporation in 1913 and gradually developed as 'Castle Hill Hospital' - these days a leading medical facility in East Yorkshire.

Thomas Thompson was clearly a man of some social conscience who was shocked by the living conditions of Cottingham's poor and determined to do something about it by copying a scheme that had been tried out in Nottingham. In 1819 he persuaded Cottingham's Overseers of the Poor to spend £20 a year on renting twelve acres of church-owned land in the east of the village. This land was then divided into twenty strips and twenty poor families were re-settled there in order to farm it at

Market Green and King Street around 1924. A motor bus owned by the Cottingham of firm of Fussey's leaves for Hull. To the right of the picture is the 'Cosy Coliseum' (later the Imperial): a cinema that operated in Cottingham between 1913 and 1929.

The impressive Church of St Mary the Virgin with its central tower and large nave (dating from the 14th century) are indications of the wealth and importance of Cottingham in the Middle Ages.

a nominal rent of two shillings per year. This innovative scheme seems to have prospered for eighteen of the tenants went on to build cottages on their strips and by 1830 this part of Cottingham was called 'New Village'.

At the historic core of the village is Hallgate which for centuries was the principal street of 'Old Cottingham' leading from the magnificent church of St Mary the Virgin to the medieval manor house (or hall) that gave the street its name. The church dates from the early 14th century and its size and splendour indicates how prosperous Cottingham was in the Middle Ages when it was the third largest place in the East Riding, after Beverley and Hull, with an estimated population, in 1377, of 1,500 people. Like many East Riding villages, Cottingham obtained the right in 1199 to hold markets and fairs by royal charter. The modern-day Thursday market held on Market Green at the heart of the village was established 1985 and is a revival after a gap of over one hundred years, of this relationship between sellers and buyers.

Cottingham, like other places close to Hull, was affected by the quarrels between King Charles the First and Parliament culminating in the Civil War of 1642-1646. The walled town and port of Hull was held by the parliamentarians and became a target for royalist forces during two sieges in 1642 and 1643. The village of Cottingham was well placed to become a royalist base for the Duke of Newcastle's army to launch their attacks on Hull's defences during the autumn of 1643. It suffered all the horrors of occupation by an unpaid army that sought to compensate themselves in other ways. In a letter of 24th October 1643 a bailiff of Cottingham wrote:

> "Misery is fallen upon us. Our horses, beasts and sheep are driven away and most of our houses plundered. We are now brought to utter ruin."

If the depredations of the soldiers were not bad enough Cottingham's residents also had to contend with a mass of women camp-followers who had followed their men folk to the battle area and robbed the inhabitants "of all their linen without any pity at all." Yet despite the efforts of the royalists the second siege of Hull was a failure and the Duke eventually ordered a retreat. However his troops carried out acts of sabotage to forestall any pursuit and also stole valuable plate from Cottingham Church.

In the more peaceful conditions of the eighteenth century Cottingham was well placed to attract newcomers from Hull's increasingly prosperous merchant class, especially with the improvement of the Newland to Cottingham road by the local turnpike trust after 1764. One of the earliest surviving examples of the residences they constructed is Snuff Mill House built by William Travis, a snuff and tobacco merchant. Snuff is ground tobacco inhaled through the nose and was extremely fashionable among the elite in Georgian England and claims were even made about its health benefits! In 1755 Travis bought Cottingham's South Mill, powered by the waters of Cottingham Beck and formerly used to mill corn and for paper-making, to grind tobacco into snuff and built the adjacent Snuff Mill House soon after.

By 1822 Cottingham had a population of 2,479 and its appeal to Hull's merchant class was shown by the writings of Edward Baines who said, "it boasts many handsome country houses, gardens and pleasure grounds" and reported that two stage coaches a day operated between the village and Hull. The attractiveness of the village for Hull's elite was given a further boost with the arrival of the railway in October 1846 for Cottingham Station lay only a short walk away from the centre of the village and journeys into Hull took just ten minutes. Even before the First World War smaller terraced houses and semi detached houses for a growing middle class were being built on existing streets like Linden Avenue and Millhouse Woods Lane as well as newly laid out streets like Exeter Street off New Village Road.

One survivor of Cottingham's wealth of grand houses from its period of rapid growth is Elm Tree House built in 1820 on a two-acre site off South Street for John Hebblewhite, a Hull draper. This imposing residence with its stone front and grand staircase was altered and enlarged in the 1860s and the opulent lifestyle of a succession of well-to-do owners is indicated by an auction of the contents when the last of them, Gunter Lacey, died in 1934. Among the lots sold at auction in December 1935 were ten bottles of claret which sold for £1 2s 6d, or about £1 12 in modern money and a gallon of whisky which realised £2 18s 0d (£2. 90).

For the past sixty years Elm Tree House has been the home of Cottingham's famous 'Memorial Club'. This had begun life in 1919 when a number of Cottingham's ex-servicemen got together to form an organisation that would commemorate those comrades who had lost their lives during the First World War and to sustain the comradeship of the survivors by providing the facilities of a first class club. One of its most

The Caravan Extravaganza held in September each year at the Lawns site of Hull University enables thousands of caravan enthusiasts to check out the latest models.

famous members was the acclaimed poet Philip Larkin (1922-1985) who was the chief librarian at the nearby University of Hull for thirty years.

Cottingham, like many villages in the East Riding, saw a large number of its young men enlist in the armed forces during World War One and many were to sacrifice their lives in the trenches of the Western Front between 1914 and 1918. A memorial to those who died stands close to Cottingham Church and it is possible to find out more about those whose names are recorded by using the database on the East Yorkshire Regiment website (www.east-yorkshire-regiment.co.uk). One of the names inscribed on the war memorial is that of Private William Pool whose mother lived on Hallgate in the village. A member of the eleventh battalion of the East Yorkshire regiment, Private Pool died of wounds received during the Battle of Arras in 1917 and is buried at the military cemetery near the village of Duisans in north-eastern France.

Another major factor in the Cottingham story has been Hull University for from its beginnings in 1927 there was a decision to house the students in Cottingham. In 1928 Thwaite House (now Thwaite Hall) and Northfields House (now Needler Hall) were purchased for this purpose and in the years that followed many more acquisitions were

100

The dramatist and screen writer Alan Plater was one of Cottingham's most famous residents. (Image courtesy of the Plater family)

made. Today these student numbers make a significant contribution to Cottingham's total population of over 17,000 people.

The university's largest site in Cottingham is the Lawns on Harland Way comprising seven halls of residence and associated facilities and built on a former military camp used by American soldiers during World War Two. Apart from the student accommodation it provides the Lawns also has associations with another of Cottingham's major activities: caravan making. In September each year the Lawns hosts the 'Caravan Extravaganza', a showcase of the latest touring models and static holiday homes. Well represented at the show is Cottingham's own caravan maker: the Swift Group based at Dunswell Road.

The story of Swift Caravans is a rags-to-riches affair since a company that in 2007 had sales of 191.3 million pounds began life in 1964 as a small operation located in a garage on Hedon Road, Hull. The company moved to Cottingham in 1970 and since then has expanded its facilities there with a training centre and a new factory complex. The Swift Group has grown to be a major force in the UK's caravan and motorhome industry and owns many of Britain's most famous caravan brands including 'Bessacarr', 'Sprite' and 'Sterling'.

Over the years Cottingham has been home to some of the area's most talented and creative people and these include the actor Brian Rix (who was born in the village in 1924), the journalist and novelist Winifred Holtby (1898-1935) and the stage and television playwright Alan Plater (1935-2010). For many years Alan Plater lived at a house on Hull Road Cottingham and he became a household name for his work on major television series like 'Z Cars' in the 1960s and 'Flambards' in the 1970s.

Cottingham, in spite of its rapid growth in the last hundred years and its close proximity to Hull, has retained its own distinctive identity and its own terrific sense of community. This is shown by the huge effort made in recent years to make Cottingham's 'Christmas Lights' the best of their type in Yorkshire. The idea sprang from a conversation between local shopkeepers in a Cottingham pub in September 1981 and a committee was formed soon after to do the planning. Initially the lights were hired from Blackpool but such was the enthusiasm for the 'Christmas Lights Project' that the decision was soon made for Cottingham to buy its own lights and install a permanent wiring system. Supported by local fund raising events including a golf tournament the 'switch on' event in late November has become an eagerly awaited and much-cherished part of the Cottingham scene.

CHAPTER 15

SPROATLEY

When people think of Sproatley, seven miles north-east of Hull, they usually bring to mind the magnificent stately home of Burton Constable situated close by. Known as the 'Treasure House of Holderness' Burton Constable is an Elizabethan mansion set in three hundred acres of beautiful parkland partly created by renowned eighteenth century landscape gardener Capability Brown. From around 1570 the house became the principal seat of the Constable family and in the centuries that followed, as the largest landowners in Sproatley, they came to dominate the lives of its people. By 1779 William Constable had around 593 acres at Sproatley and the family's purchase of other farms as they became available meant that by 1912 their holdings had grown to 934 acres. The historian George Poulson writing in the nineteenth century said of Sproatley:

> "The village is the resort of many whom business or pleasure take to Burton Constable."

Yet the origins of Sproatley pre-date the Constable family's presence in the village. In the early 11th century its name was 'Sprotele' and is thought to be derived from a word meaning a 'clearing where brushwood grows'. The original core of the village stood on higher ground close to the church of St Swithin and even by the eighteenth century development elsewhere had hardly begun.

The creation of the Hull to Hedon turnpike trust in 1745 and the improvement of local roads probably helped to stimulate more passing trade on the route to Aldborough and it seems that the two village pubs, the 'Blue Bell' and the 'Constable Arms', built in the late eighteenth century helped to cater for this need. In the nineteenth century the 'Blue Bell' was described as a 'posting house' and its stables would have provided fresh horses for the omnibus that plied between the King's Head in Witham (Hull) and Aldborough while the inn provided refreshment to weary travellers. In the nineteenth century, as now, publicans had to deal with intoxicated and unruly customers and a document held in the East Riding Archive dated January 16th 1846 records a complaint made by the 'Blue Bell' licensee John Pexton that on the previous Saturday:

The Blue Bell Inn around 1910 with cricketers gathered for a group photograph. Sproatley Cricket Club had been founded around 1897. (Image courtesy of www.paul-gibson.com)

"Henry Fussey did violently and unlawfully assault and shake him."

The document required the constable of Sproatley to summon Fussey to appear before local magistrates on Monday 2nd February at 11am to answer the complaint.

Close to the 'Blue Bell' at the eastern edge of the village is the former Sproatley Police Station and courthouse built in 1849 on a site given by Sir Clifford Constable. In the census of 1851 Anthony Coulthard was named as the superintendent of police and he lived there with his wife Ann. Sworn to uphold the law Coulthard was soon to fall foul of it himself in a remarkable civil case heard at the York Assizes in July 1852.

Coulthard's problems began when he arrested a local man called William Johnson, a labourer living at the village of Withernwick about four miles from Sproatley who occasionally travelled "about the country with a horse and cart to gather rags and bones." In November 1851 Johnson had been at the annual hiring fair for servants in nearby Hedon but on his way home had stopped at a public house in the village of Marton for a drink with four or five other men. Disturbed from his slumber around midnight the publican, John Wright refused to serve them. Wright was to allege that he saw Johnson in his garden breaking one large earthenware pot and stealing another but that this had been returned to him a few days later.

By the 23rd November Superintendent Coulthard had received a letter from Wright telling him what had happened and two days later had apprehended and arrested Johnson on a charge of stealing the pot. According to Coulthard he had allowed the Withernwick man to return home with his horse and cart on the understanding that Johnson would give himself up to face justice. In the event Johnson failed to appear and so Coulthard went looking for him and arrested him, for a second time, at a public house in Withernwick on the 27th November. Johnson was taken to the Sproately lock-up for the night and then the next day to the home of Robert Harrison, a local landowner and magistrate, at Benninghome seven miles away.

Having heard Coulthard's account Harrison decided that Johnson should not be prosecuted for larceny but for vagrancy and with being a rogue and a vagabond in that he had "wandered abroad in the streets" and had been in Wright's garden for an unlawful purpose. There seems to have been a degree of informality about the whole proceedings with the case being considered in Johnson's absence. It was said that Johnson had

105

Burton Constable Hall, near Sproatley, is one of East Yorkshire's most famous stately homes and dates from 1570 (This image is from 'A Series of Picturesque Views of Seats of Noblemen and Gentlemen of Great Britain and Ireland' courtesy of the Noel collection at www.jamessmithnoelcollection.org)

been placed in the saddle room of the magistrate's home before being led across the yard where he was met by Harrison who told him " I have a charge against you for disturbing John Wright from his night's rest and for your so doing I shall send you to the Beverley House of Correction for twenty one days with hard labour."

On his release Johnson sought legal advice and lawyers acting for him were to allege that his detention and imprisonment had been unlawful because among other things Coulthard had not obtained an arrest warrant beforehand. An action for trespass was then begun against both the Sproatley policeman and the magistrate. In one document Johnson claimed that he had been treated "with great force and violence" and had been placed in handcuffs and manacles before being tied by Coulthard to the strings of a saddle and dragged by the superintendent's horse to Sproatley police station. He also alleged that "he had never been before the magistrate" suggesting that Harrison had not troubled himself with due legal process. At the trial in July 1852 Johnson was also to claim that during his imprisonment at Beverley he had been subjected to "a great many indignities" and since we know that the prison made use of a treadmill to make criminals undergo 'hard labour' this was probably true.

Johnson's likely purpose in taking legal action against the wealthy JP Robert Harrison was, in the words of one lawyer, that of "extorting money from him" and from the evidence of legal papers we know that he was seeking £250 in compensation. To counter the claim that Johnson was the injured party it is interesting that lawyers acting for Harrison had prepared some accusations of their own. In one brief it said:

> "Johnson is in the habit of leading a loose life and goes travelling about the country with a horse and cart under the colour of buying rags and bones. He is suspected of being a poacher and is known to local gamekeepers."

In the event the judge dismissed the charge against the East Riding JP saying that although Harrison "had acted very injudiciously he had done nothing wrong to prejudice him in the eyes of his countrymen." While the judge was unwilling to act against an important local landowner and magistrate like Harrison whose reputation mattered it was a different story for Coulthard, a man of more humble origins. Coulthard had been an agricultural labourer before becoming a policeman and the verdict of the court went against him. Johnson was awarded £5 in

The police station and magistrates court was erected here in 1849.

compensation plus costs for the 'trespass' committed against him by Coulthard.

Anthony Coulthard was soon in trouble again for on the 2nd May 1854 a summons was issued against him on behalf of George Bell a labourer from Elsternwick alleging assault and false imprisonment. By 1861 he was no longer a policeman and had left East Yorkshire. The Census of that year shows he was now living in Northumberland and was employed as the 'Idiots Warden' at the Newcastle-upon-Tyne Union Workhouse.

Meanwhile the Police Station at Sproatley remained in use until 1970 and the magistrates continued to meet at the courthouse until 1995. In a directory of 1921 Lieutenant Colonel Chichester Constable was named as the Chairman of the Bench while eight other important East Riding citizens also served as magistrates to hear cases of lawbreaking in Middle Holderness. The minute books of the magistrates held by the East Riding Archive make interesting reading and record minor misdemeanours that would seldom be heard by a court today. On the 7th

March 1951, for example, the Sproatley magistrates fined William Love ten shillings (50p) for riding his bicycle at night with no rear light.

In addition to its police station/courthouse Sproatley also saw other building work taking place in the older part of the village in the mid nineteenth century: a new school was built in 1868 incorporating houses for the master and mistress. Sproatley was an endowed school with money coming from the will of Bridget Biggs (1733), the daughter of a seventeenth century rector of the village. She had bequeathed the income from several small farms in the Sheffield area to support the school and in 1892 this and another endowment was providing an income of over £300 a year. However just because the school was relatively wealthy did not guarantee a good education for the seventy or so children registered to attend. When the East Riding County Council began inspecting Sproatley Endowed Church of England School in 1922 many of the reports were damning. Gilbert Thompson, assisted by his wife, was the Head of the school and in October 1922 the inspector wrote:

"I have never met a person so wanting in humour, capacity to see things as they really are, or any apparent sense of his own human imperfections as this man. He does not discern that his children are bored to death."

By way of illustration the inspector then went on to describe in great detail a thirty-minute lesson on the 'human hand' given by Thompson in which the children were:

"Solemnly taught that the hand has a front, a back, a palm and knuckles and some joints that could move. There was not a word about tendons or muscles. Yet although the children had learned nothing that they had not known before Mr Thompson finished the lesson, to which I had listened with great fortitude throughout, with an air of modest triumph."

The inspector was equally unimpressed by the teaching of arithmetic when he gave the children this task:

"A boy has 37 marbles, wins 29 and then loses 39. How many has he?"

The inspector recorded that only three children out of eighteen got it right and that the great majority of pupils had added the three numbers together!

Summing up the Headmaster's failings the inspector concluded:

> "So much of what is done in the upper school is simply not worthwhile. All the majority of Thompson's psychology is directed to teaching the children what they already know or what they needn't learn."

Comments by a second East Riding inspector, Mr J Moffat, were critical of the school throughout the 1920s and 1930s. On the 2nd April 1925 he wrote:

> "Mr Thompson is somewhat weak in personality and he seems to have an unreasonably high opinion of his own capabilities. The bulk of the pupils are sleepy and unresponsive and the teaching is dull."

These days Head Teachers are frequently held to account for the failings of their schools but is interesting to note that this "weak and dull teacher" as Moffat described him in May 1938 remained in post despite the criticisms.

In common with most East Riding villages Sproatley has seen rapid change since the Second World War and is now a popular commuter settlement for people working in Hull. This influx of newcomers has probably been a major factor in raising pupil aspirations and the fortunes of Sproatley Endowed Church of England School have been radically transformed in recent years.

By the time of the 2001 census Sproatley had a population of 1,353 (compared to just 325 in 1891) and this reflects the appeal of the village in recent times. Yet while the village has seen much new house building in the last fifty years this ancient Holderness settlement retains much of its old world charm and character through the creation of a conservation area in 1987. As many visitors to Burton Constable have discovered Sproatley is a village worth exploring in its own right.

CHAPTER 16

NAFFERTON

The village of Nafferton lies about two miles north-east of Driffield and is situated at the southern edge of the Yorkshire Wolds. Archaeological evidence suggests that there was human activity in the area around 4000BC, during the Stone Age, although the settlement of Nafferton itself probably dates from the 9th or 10th century AD.

For centuries farming was the major economic activity of the villages of East Yorkshire and Nafferton was really no different to scores of other villages in the county in this respect. In fact the name of the village is partly derived from "ton" a word used by Angles (a Germanic tribe who settled in the East Riding from the fifth century) to mean "a farm". However the first part of the name is thought to have come from another group of invaders, the Scandinavians and probably refers to an individual called 'Nafftar' (the night traveller) of whom we know nothing. However, the presence of an Anglo-Saxon community in the Nafferton area has been confirmed by the discovery of a number of their cemeteries the first of which was found in 1845.

The Norman conquest of 1066 would probably have made little difference to the lives of the ordinary folk of the village even though ownership of the land changed hands. At the time of the Domesday Book (1086) the largest of these landowners was William de Percy who controlled about 3,360 acres. However for ordinary villagers their daily routine would have altered little in the centuries that followed and their work would have been ruled by the changing seasons: the need to sow seed, to look after and harvest their crops as well as to take care of their animals. The Church of All Saints standing on a high bank and dominating the village at a place where four roads join would have met their spiritual needs.

Close by was the village lock-up, the stocks and the pinfold. A pinfold was an enclosed area where stray animals were rounded up and kept if their owners failed to supervise them. In order to secure their release a fine had to be paid but sometimes this led to friction between the owner and the pinder, the official who supervised the strays. A document held by the East Riding Archive in Beverley tells of one such incident in July 1791 when Robert Wilson of Nafferton violently assaulted the pinder, Thomas Coates, in order to 'rescue' his two asses from the pound.

Nafferton Mere was created or enlarged to provide a plentiful supply for village water mills. A water mill was first recorded in the Domesday Book of 1086. The last mill and the maltings were demolished in 1985 to make way for housing.

H Kitching and Sons (Motor Engineers) is a family run business and stands on the site of a former blacksmith's shop.

A local magistrate issued a warrant for the arrest of Wilson and at his trial in October 1791 he was sentenced to a month in prison.

Another feature of the village scene overlooked by the church and still very much a focal point of the Nafferton of today is a large pond or mere. Fed by springs, Nafferton Mere was created to be a millpond to turn water wheels at mills close by. A new corn mill and maltings, built in 1840, were once important local industries and used to turn locally grown barley into malt for the brewing industry. The massive six story buildings once dominated the village but were demolished in 1985 to make way for new housing.

For a farming community like Nafferton one of the most important changes for property owners came in 1772 with the enclosure of the open fields and commons and their replacement by compact holdings of land and field patterns resembling those of today. Of the lives of the ordinary village folk of the time we know a little from a rare survival in the East Riding Archive. A letter of March 1777 from Thomas Bowness, the vicar of Nafferton, to the East Riding landowner and JP

John Grimston tells of the marital discord of two of his parishioners: Roger Walker and his wife Lydia. The two were being supported financially by the parish but were living apart with Lydia, who was referred to by the vicar as the Queen of Scolds, refusing to "live quietly and peaceably with her husband" unless one of his women friends was removed from out of the neighbourhood! The vicar described Roger Walker as an "old shifty rascal" and his estranged wife as a "nuisance" but promised to "keep them as quiet as we can".

By the beginning of the nineteenth century the population of Nafferton parish stood at around 900 people and a trade directory of 1823 listed sixteen people described as farmers/yeomen along with a host of other trades (like blacksmiths, bricklayers, carpenters, shoemakers and tailors) typical of any self-contained rural community of the time. In common with many other East Riding villages of the nineteenth century there was a growing interest in providing an education for its children and in 1845 a National School (supported by the Church of England) was built on High Street. In the 1870s and the 1880s the village was to become the setting for both tragedy and scandal with the suicide of one schoolmaster in 1874 and the arrest of another in 1883 on a charge of plotting the murders of two of his former pupils!

On November 24th 1874 a local newspaper reported that the head of the school for the previous fifteen years, Robert Southwick had hung himself. Two local men, alerted by his daughter after he failed to return home, broke into the school and found his body suspended from a beam behind the blackboard and easel. A newspaper report of the tragedy suggested that Mr Southwick had been suffering from depression after his son had been committed to an asylum with mental health problems.

In September 1883 it was the turn of another Nafferton schoolmaster, Francis Randall, to make the headlines in a bizarre case reported by a local newspaper of the time. It was at first alleged that Randall had tried to persuade John Smith, a Hull fisherman visiting Nafferton in search of work, to murder on his behalf Sarah Jane Bell and John Kilvington. The two intended victims were probably sweethearts and both of them had been former pupils of Nafferton National School. From the start Smith had pretended to go along with plan but had secretly made contact with the Driffield police who then kept watch and gathered evidence.

By the time the case was heard fully in October 1883 the more serious charge of 'incitement to murder' had been dropped and instead Randall was charged with "unlawfully inciting John Smith to inflict

The village hall was built in 1946 and provides a valuable space for community activities.

grievous bodily harm on Sarah Jane Bell." From the evidence presented at his trial it seems that the forty-eight year old schoolmaster had become seriously infatuated with his fifteen-year old former pupil and, despite having a wife and two grown up daughters, had tried to persuade the parents of the girl to let him take their daughter "to a foreign country." At the trial it was suggested that having failed to persuade Sarah's parents to go along with his 'elopement plan' he had decided to seize the girl by force with the aid of Smith. The evidence of the parents and that of Nafferton policeman PC Sharp, who said he had seen Randall give John Smith a payment of 2s 0d (10p) together with a stout walking stick to carry out the assault, helped to seal the schoolmaster's fate. The jury returned a verdict of guilty but their request for mercy may have helped in reducing Randall's sentence to one of twelve months imprisonment. For his actions in alerting the police to the planned crime John Smith received a reward of 10s 0d (50p).

By the time Bulmer's Directory of Nafferton was published in 1892 William Preston was the master of the National School and this

North Street Nafferton on a Spring Day. A byass to avoid the village was created in 1927.

same directory lists a miscellany of other trades including drapers, dressmakers, saddlers and blacksmiths needed to serve a population that had grown to 1,295 people. While many of these businesses have disappeared others have evolved to provide more up-to-date services for the local community. One of these is H Kitchen and Sons a motor engineering business that developed on the site of a former blacksmith's shop. Ian Kitchen now owns the business but when his grandfather bought it in the 1920s shoeing horses and repairing agricultural implements was still an important activity. It was in the 1940s and 1950s that Ian's father and grandfather turned increasingly to the motor trade.

With a population today of over 2000 people Nafferton is one of the larger communities in the East Riding and it saw much new house building both before and after the Second World War. In the 1960s for example a new estate was built in the former grounds of Nafferton Hall attracting those from Driffield and further afield. The village website indicates just what a busy place it has become and how those who have moved here in recent years have quickly been welcomed as valuable members of a thriving community.

CHAPTER 17

LECONFIELD

The village of Leconfield, three miles north of Beverley is unusual in the East Riding for it has a military tradition dating back to the fourteenth century. Once the site of Leconfield Castle, the home of one of England's most powerful families in the Middle Ages, these days the village is home to the Defence School of Transport a facility of national importance in the training of Britain's armed services.

Anyone who regularly travels on the roads of East Yorkshire will have seen large numbers of lorries and other vehicles of the Defence School of Transport based at Normandy Barracks, Leconfield. The DST is probably the largest driver training school in the world with over 14,000 personnel from the army, the Royal Air Force and the Royal Marines being trained each year. In fact Leconfield's long association with Britain's modern armed forces began in 1936 when an RAF airfield opened there occupying over a thousand acres and helping to swell the population of this formerly tiny village in the years that followed.

The origins of Leconfield seem to go back to Anglo-Saxon times and the name is thought by some to be derived from "land belonging to those dwelling by the stream." The oldest part of the village was probably around the Church of St Catherine on Arram Road and worship at the site dates back to at least the ninth century. In the Domesday Book of 1086 the village was called Lachinfield and by the 14th century the patronage of the Lord of the Manor, Henry de Percy, had secured a weekly market and an annual fair for its residents.

In fact the importance of Leconfield in the Middle Ages owed much to the presence of the wealthy and important Percy family (the Earls of Northumberland) who created a fortified manor house and deer park to the southwest of the village and this became one of their principal residences. The late Middle Ages was a turbulent time in England and the Percy family like other members of the peerage were involved in the Wars of the Roses between the Lancastrian and Yorkist claimants to the throne. The third Earl of Northumberland, who was born at Leconfield, was one of the estimated 28,000 people killed in 1461 at the Battle of Towton, two miles from Tadcaster, one of the bloodiest battles ever fought on British soil.

The Church of St Catherine in Arram Road. Parts of the church date back to Norman times. It was closed for two and a half years (2005-2008) after dry rot was discovered and services were held in the village hall. £60,000 was secured through local fundraising and an English Heritage grant for restoration work on this ancient building.

King Henry VIII and his fifth wife Catherine Howard were visitors to Leconfield Castle in 1541.

Despite these upheavals life at Leconfield 'Castle' continued to dominate the village until the late 16th century and the household was said to consist of one hundred and sixty six persons together with around fifty-five guests each day. One of these was the Tudor king Henry the Eighth who stayed there with his fifth wife Catherine Howard and their attendants in 1541. Surrounded by a moat it was described by one 16th century commentator as a large house built largely of timber but partly of brick and stone. Unfortunately the political misfortunes of the Percy family helped to bring a decline of their power and their 'castle' at Leconfield, after falling into decay, was demolished in the early seventeenth century. However the dry moat, surrounding the four-acre site, can still be seen to remind us of the former importance of the place.

In the centuries that followed Leconfield, in common with all East Riding villages, would have been dominated by the needs of farming and in a directory of 1823 ten farmers were named. One of them, Thomas Moss, was also the licensee of 'The Roebuck' on the High Road through the village while another public house was 'The Bay Horse' where Mary Sellers was described as the 'victualer'. This was still there in 1857 when Thomas Fields was recorded as the licensee and he also worked as the village blacksmith. Yet by the 1870s Leconfield had no public house at all and it is unusual in the East Riding in that, despite its size, it remains a 'dry' village to this day, although a social club opened in 1986.

By the mid-nineteenth century the population of Leconfield was three hundred and sixty two people and like many other East Riding villages provision was soon made for the education of its children. In 1858 a church school with a master's house was built on Arram Road for fifty children and supported by voluntary contributions from residents and from Lord Leconfield and Lord Hotham. Living there at the time of the 1881 census was the schoolmaster, Robert Topham, who was born in Woodmansey, his wife and their six children.

When the East Riding inspector visited Leconfield School in the early 1920s some of his reports were critical of the teaching he found there. Between February 1921 and October 1924 there were four different head teachers and of the first of these, Miss Horn, he was to write:

> "The Headmistress is too easy going. Very little thought seems to have been given to the schemes of work and to the preparation of lessons. Daily work seems to be more in the nature of filling in time rather than in serious teaching."

Farming was once the main occupation of the village. Shown here are Leconfield farm workers with a portable steam threshing machine around the year 1904. (Image courtesy of the East Riding Museums Service)

According to the inspector her replacement, Mrs Williamson, was self confident and vigorous but was eccentric and had "foolish delusions of grandeur". She was soon at loggerheads with the vicar and seems to have resented his intrusive behaviour. The inspector wrote in 1922:

> "They are not good friends at present. Probably there are faults on both sides. Reading between the lines I should say that he has probably made efforts to take an interest in Mrs Williamson's domestic affairs and guide her in the way she should go. Mrs Williamson has most likely been rude to him."

Within months the vicar was claiming that at least two of the other managers of the school were of the opinion that she was "not suitable for the position she holds." Yet it is interesting to note that the inspector did not seem to share this opinion for he stated that Leconfield School had improved, that the Headmistress was working conscientiously and the children were beginning to show more effort.

Yet given her poor relationship with the vicar it is not surprising that by November 1923 she was gone and had been replaced by another short-lived appointment. The inspector said of her:

> "Miss Carter is a superior kind of woman. She gives the impression of being somewhat neurotic but appears to have high ideals."

The difficulties and tensions of running Leconfield's small church school, with four head mistresses in only three years, may have had more to do with the personality of the vicar than anything else. The inspector reported that the fourth appointment, Miss Wright, who arrived in April 1924, was the best of the four he had seen and that under her "the children have improved steadily" Yet within a short time she was at odds with the elderly school cleaner since he "resented taking orders from a young girl". The inspector reported that the cleaner was also the vicar's handyman and enjoyed the vicar's support.

By October 1937 Leconfield School had just thirty-five children on roll but the major changes happening to the village at that time were reflected by an inspection report that said: "an influx of fifteen children is expected from the aerodrome next week." RAF Leconfield had opened on the 3rd December 1936 and began life as part of Bomber Command. At the outbreak of the Second World War planes from the base dropped propaganda leaflets over Germany. By October 1939 Leconfield had been taken over by Fighter Command whose pilots used its grass airstrip to rest and regroup after periods of action during the Battle of Britain in 1940. The presence of the airfield made Leconfield an important target for the Luftwaffe too and records in the East Riding Archive in Beverley give details of two raids in 1940-1941. On the 27th October 1940 five high-explosive bombs were dropped on the base. Although it was reported that damage was "negligible", there was one casualty: a Polish airman serving with 302 Squadron. The Germans made a more determined effort in May 1941 when 23 high explosive and 250 incendiary bombs missed their intended target and fell on Leconfield Grange Farm instead.

In October 1941 RAF Leconfield was reconstructed as a heavy bomber base with concrete runways being laid and the years 1942-1945 saw numerous raids by Wellington and Halifax bombers over Nazi occupied Europe. Even after the war the station continued in use as a jet

An army vehicle being put through its paces inside the Defence School of Transport at Leconfield. (Image courtesy of the DST)

fighter base, finally closing in 1976 and to this day the RAF maintains a presence here with its search and rescue helicopters providing cover over the North Sea from the Wash to Hartlepool.

In 1977 Leconfield's new role as an Army School of Mechanical Transport began and its fleet of Bedford trucks soon becoming a familiar sight on the roads of East Yorkshire; almost twenty years later RAF and Royal Marine driver training also moved here. The Defence School of Transport is now regarded as the 'Centre for Excellence' for driver training in the UK providing ninety-five different courses and using a fleet of one thousand two hundred vehicles. The range of vehicles that the DST has at its disposal is remarkable: from saloon cars and motorcycles to specialist military light goods vehicles. The base also has sixteen kilometres of road training circuits including a purpose-built hill, roundabouts and junctions to help trainees to develop basic road sense and driving skills before they venture out onto public roads. To simulate the kind of harsh driving conditions to be found in some parts of the world there are also eighteen kilometres of cross country circuits with obstacles like water crossings to test both vehicles and drivers.

The commandant of the Leconfield facility when asked about the role of the DST in the United Kindom's defence said:

> "Every driver, operator and vehicle manager in the three armed services is either trained here, trained by an instructor from here or trained by a contract set and managed from here. The role is a key one, and we take it very seriously indeed."

Like many East Riding communities Leconfield has seen a rapid development in recent times with plenty of new house building on both sides of the busy A164 road that passes through it. Yet although the village, like many others, has become a popular commuter settlement for Hull and Beverley its growth began much earlier than elsewhere. The significance of a 'military presence' in the Leconfield story is apparent from the population statistics for in 1931 there were only 283 people living in the parish. In 1951, just fifteen years after the establishment of RAF Leconfield, the census recorded a population of 1,538 and by 2001 this had risen still further to 1,990.

CHAPTER 18

PATRINGTON

For anyone who regularly heads east to the coast from Hull the village of Patrington will be a familiar sight since it lies on the A1033 road to Withernsea, four miles away. Although these days it is classed as a village Patrington in the early nineteenth century was described as a 'market town' and thanks to its links to the Humber via Patrington Haven had a thriving trade in corn and coal with the West Riding.

As the name suggests Patrington probably had its origins in Anglo-Saxon times for 'ton' is an Old English word meaning farm or hamlet while 'Pat' is derived from the Church of St Patrick. The church, which dates back to the 14th century and long known as the Queen of Holderness because of its size and splendour, remains the most distinguishing feature of this important Holderness community and dominates the surrounding flat countryside. Back in 1823 the journalist Edward Baines said of the church spire soaring one hundred and ninety feet into the sky: "this has long been a landmark for seamen on entering the Humber"

Although throughout much of its history Patrington was, like any other East Riding community, dominated by the needs of farming the importance of the sea in its growth should not be under-estimated. A creek called Patrington Haven lay about a mile from this busy Holderness community and Baines said "the inhabitants used to boast of the former excellence of their harbour". While he conceded that Patrington Haven was now silting-up he also revealed that "several vessels trade to Hull and London with corn and many vessels are employed in the coal and lime trade with the West Riding." A directory of 1834 recorded the names of nine individuals resident at Patrington Haven and described as 'coal and lime merchants' and a further three people who were 'corn merchants'. By the mid nineteenth century the fishing industry also had a base here although by 1892 it was reported that "there is not now a sufficient depth of water to permit the landing of the fishing smacks" and that the smack owners, although still resident in the town, had to make use of facilities further away at Stone Creek.

In fact the haven was no longer used by shipping after 1869 but long before then the build-up of silt had made it obvious that it did not have a long-term future. The coal and corn trade of Patrington Haven thus

The Queen of Holderness (the Church of St Patrick) dates from the 14th century and remains an important local landmark and visitor attraction.

became a target of a new proposal in 1852 for a railway to link the village with Hull. The Hull and Holderness Railway was the brainchild of Alderman Anthony Bannister, a Hull businessman and politician, and aimed to capitalise on the need to provide Patrington with a more efficient mode of transport than by water or road as well as to develop Withernsea as a seaside resort.

As a thriving community with a weekly market and three fairs each year Patrington attracted a wide range of occupations like

Patrington Windmill around 1900. According to a directory of 1892, James Appleby was the miller. (Image courtesy of the East Riding Museum Service)

139

blacksmiths, shoe makers, milliners, tin-plate workers and saddlers and it has been estimated that by the early nineteenth century sixty percent of its population of 1244 people in 1823, were engaged in trade or manufacture.

An important boost to the local economy came in 1846 when William Marshall became Lord of the Manor for he leased some of his land to his two brothers from Leeds to build a flax mill at Patrington in 1848. This continued in business until 1883 employing, at the height of its success, 150 people many of them Irish immigrants. It is an indication of the prosperity of Patrington that it soon had its own gas works built by the Provincial Gaslight and Coke Company who manufactured gas from coal and supplied the Flax Company, the public houses and the residents alike and enabled the town to have its street lamps lit by gas. Another of the Gas Company's customers was the local Poor Law Union and a document in the East Riding Archive dated the 12th February 1877 records a payment of £13 3s 8d (£13.19) by its clerk, Abraham Dunn, for gas.

In the early nineteenth century Patrington had its own poor house and a list of the rules of this institution from 1807, survives in the East Riding Archive. Like all parishes of that time Patrington's ratepayers were responsible for the maintenance of their own paupers who because of factors like unemployment, ill health or old age could not support themselves. The social stigma of being a pauper was perhaps made worse by a rule that stated:

> "every person receiving parochial relief shall wear on his or her clothing the badge or letters of Patrington Poor –PP."

After the passing of the 1834 Poor Law Amendment Act Patrington became the centre of twenty-six parishes in Holderness that had joined together in a Poor Law Union to build a new workhouse. This rather forbidding building was completed in 1838 and was to designed to house up to 175 paupers including orphans, the mentally-deficient, the sick, the able-bodied poor and the elderly. The original aim of the workhouse system was to deter all but the most desperate from applying to the parish for assistance. Typically life in the workhouse was made deliberately unpleasant with a meagre diet, like oatmeal porridge, monotonous work such as stone-breaking and harsh regulations to keep order and remind inmates of their lowly status.

A punishment book from the days of the workhouse survives in the East Riding Archive in Beverley and records both the misdemeanours of the inmates and the penalties they suffered. The first entry in the book of 23rd January 1847, concerned Mary Andrew who was accused of "ill-treating her own infant" and was sent to Beverley Gaol for twenty-one days as a punishment. A year later she was in trouble again for her general bad behaviour and it was ordered that she be kept in solitary confinement for forty-eight hours.

For troublesome pauper children physical punishment could sometimes be used and an entry of 4th December 1879 records that Susanah Boys was "flogged by the matron of the workhouse for her dirty habits". In 1895 two young brothers, Arthur and Robert Dunn, who quarrelled in the dining hall at suppertime were caned by the workhouse master.

Given the harsh nature of the workhouse regime it is not surprising that some inmates tried to abscond and from the punishment book we learn about Jane Richardson who in February 1852 "got over the yard wall" and was absent for some hours. She repeated this offence on three further occasions between March and May before being sentenced to a month in Beverley Gaol in June 1852 for absconding with two other female inmates.

The range of punishments inflicted by the Board of Guardians for infringements of the workhouse rules ranged from a simple 'admonishment' to a day's diet of 'bread and water'. Census records are particularly revealing about the people who lived at the Patrington workhouse and the 1851 census shows that of the seventy-five inmates sixteen were orphans aged five to eleven and nine were unmarried mothers with their seventeen children. At the time of the 1881 census there were 59 residents in the workhouse ranging from Annie Hardcastle from Patrington, aged two, to eighty-three year old Elizabeth Marritt from Ottringham.

The Board Of Guardians, who supervised the system of poor relief, was an unpaid body of men who met fortnightly to consider requests for assistance but they were helped in their work by a number of paid officials including a relieving officer, several assistant overseers and a number of medical practitioners. One of these was William Coates, a GP who arrived in Patrington in 1891, took up residence at 'Bleak House' and eventually became the medical officer at the workhouse itself. Here he would treat sick inmates and provide them with the medication they required. As an improvement to the institution a new infirmary with eighteen beds was opened in 1903. Coates became a well-known figure around Patrington, took a keen interest in local affairs, became a County

Dr William Coates (around 1907). Dressed in the uniform of an East Riding Volunteer he is about to climb into his 10hp Humber runabout.

Councillor and was one of the first people in the village to own a motorcar.

After the introduction of the Welfare State institutional care for the poor was no longer needed and this local workhouse closed in 1948 and was later used as a potato crisp factory before being demolished in 1981. Other changes to the village also become apparent in the years after the Second World War and in common with other Holderness communities Patrington lost its train service in 1964 with the closure of the Hull to Withernsea railway line. However around Patrington's ancient market place the village still retains an impressive range of shops and services including a bank, a post office, a butchers shop, a fish and chip shop, a bakery, and a convenience store.

One of the other notable businesses located in the Market Place is Frank Hill and Son, Auctioneers and Valuers, who moved here in 1972. The business was originally founded at Easington in the 1920s and it is still involved in the animal auction business at the East Riding's sole remaining cattle market at Dunswell. Since moving to Patrington Frank Hill and Son has also branched out into estate agency and building services work.

Patrington's Cricket Team in action during the 2008 season. (Image courtesy of Colin Brammer / Patrington Cricket Club)

Another advantage of living in the village, in the summer months at least, is the opportunity to watch Patrington Cricket Club in action at their Southside ground. The club's history dates back to the mid-nineteenth century and today it has three adult teams that play in the East Yorkshire Cricket Alliance Leagues and an under 15's team that plays in the Junior League.

For day-trippers heading out to the Holderness coast and places like Spurn Point and Withernsea, Patrington is definitely a place to halt their journey in order to explore this ancient settlement on foot. With a magnificent church, a historic manor house, old cottages and farmhouses there are many clues such as date stones, to help today's visitor to explore the heritage of this fascinating Holderness settlement.

CHAPTER 19

NORTH CAVE

The growth of private motoring since the Second World War and improvements to the road network has meant that we now take for granted fast journey times between Hull and outlying villages like North Cave. In the early nineteenth century North Cave was on the tortuous route out of Hull via Hessle and Ferriby to Thorne and stagecoaches stopped here so that exhausted horses could be changed and weary travellers could obtain refreshment. A newspaper advertisement from 1835 said:

> "A coach leaves the White Hart, North Cave every morning at quarter-past seven and arrives at the Black Horse, Carr Lane, Hull at half-past nine."

Although this horse-drawn 'four inside post-coach' travelled via South Cave, Brantingham, Welton, Ferriby and Hessle its journey time of two and a quarter hours is in marked contrast to today's trip of about thirty minutes. The coming of railways from 1840 helped to speed up travel in the East Riding and led to a greater mobility for many villagers though North Cave had to wait until 1885 and the opening of the Hull and Barnsley Railway before it had its own station.

The name of North Cave (like its near neighbour, South Cave, two miles away) is thought to be derived from the old English word *caf* meaning swift or quick for one of the most appealing features of this unspoilt East Yorkshire village is the beck that flows through it. In former times this stream was used to drive water mills at three sites and village footpaths enable today's visitor to admire the Upper Mill with its picturesque millpond. The present building dates from 1730 and a sale notice of 1821 in the East Riding Archive, claimed that the mill was situated on such an excellent stream that "it may be greatly enlarged." Another of North Cave's water-powered mills manufactured paper and a directory of 1823 records the presence of John Craggs, paper-maker.

In many ways North Cave was a hive of industry in its recent past for in the nineteenth century and for much of the twentieth the village supported a number of trades typical of a rural community where farming was the main occupation. One of these was the foundry in Church Street

The picturesque beck that flows through the village once powered three water mills here.

The Black Swan in Church Street was in existence in 1787 and rebuilt in 1813 by Thomas Dean. The inn is reputedly haunted and it is said that the ghost of a middle-aged lady in Victorian dress can be seen on the upper floor.

near where 'Old Forge House' stands today. Tom Henry Hicks who manufactured and repaired ploughs and farm implements and made fire grates, drain covers and other iron goods operated the foundry from 1897 and this was a long established business in North Cave, continuing until 1979.

Another resident of Church Street was William Alfred Gelder born in 1854, the son of a joiner and wheelwright. Educated at the village school he seemed set to follow in his father's footsteps but his ambitions were such that he moved to Hull and from 1878 began a successful career as an architect. The firm of Gelder and Kitchen grew prosperous on the commissions they received for design work on flour mills, oil seed crushing mills, and civic improvements. The name of North Cave's most illustrious son became famous throughout Hull for his reconstruction schemes in the city centre and a broad new thoroughfare was named Alfred Gelder Street in his honour. After a successful career in local politics during which he became Lord Mayor of Hull five times he was knighted in 1903 and became a Member of Parliament in 1910.

Alfred Gelder represented an upwardly mobile North Cave resident who through intelligence, ambition and hard work became rich and successful but there were many others who fared less well. For those who were unable or unwilling to work, through sickness, unemployment or old age, life could be extremely tough. In the last resort paupers could look to the overseers of the poor in North Cave for support and in the early nineteenth century the village had its own workhouse with rules strictly enforced by local magistrates. From records in the East Riding Archive, for example, we learn of the conviction in November 1833 of Sarah Wyvell who had departed the workhouse and thereby "wilfully disobeyed the lawful orders of Anthony Thompson, the governor."

After 1834 North Cave paupers came under the jurisdiction of the Howden Poor Law Union but the strict rules and a desire to keep the cost of poor relief to local taxpayers as low as possible continued as before. In March 1839 for example the Poor Law Guardians asked for action to be taken against William James Ward of Hull, gardener, for the maintenance of "Teresa Watson, a female bastard child of Mary Watson, born on the 11th December 1837 and chargeable to North Cave."

For those who could work but chose not to do so, thereby making the parish responsible for the upkeep of dependents, the Board of Guardians could also make life unpleasant. An entry in the Guardians' Minute books dated 9th January 1841 ordered that:

> "William Fallowfield be taken by the constable of North Cave before a magistrate for refusing to work and to maintain his family."

This desire to save money was also shown in correspondence dated March 27th 1849 between the Guardians and the Overseer of the Poor of Market Weighton. This letter refused reimbursement of money given by the parish of Market Weighton to a former North Cave resident, Susannah Scott, because:

> "the ratepayers of North Cave object to such repayment being made."

135

The wheelwrights shop of Saunders and Hicks around 1900. Thomas Hicks was also captain of the North Cave Fire Brigade and one of six volunteer firemen; the fire engine was kept at the foundry.

Like most East Riding villages in recent times North Cave has undergone considerable change with the disappearance of many businesses that were no longer viable when increasing car ownership and changing fashions brought more competition from shops further away. However two of the village pubs, the 'Black Swan' and the 'White Hart' mentioned in a trade directory of 1823, are still there today even though the shoemakers, drapers, tailors and fellmongers of former times have now disappeared. The 'Black Swan' in Church Street was in existence in 1787 and was rebuilt in 1813 by Thomas Dean. The inn is reputedly haunted and it is said that the ghost of a middle-aged lady in Victorian dress can be seen on the upper floor.

Long time North Cave resident Ernie Coates commented on how the village has changed dramatically in his lifetime by saying:

"There were once sixteen shops in the village including a saddlers and a bakery. What is now the Londis store was once a pork butcher's shop and it had its own slaughterhouse at the rear."

While some businesses have disappeared new opportunities have presented themselves. One of these is the 'North Cave Wetlands' an important reserve for breeding, migrating and wintering birds in the southern part of the village. Originally the site was a commercial sand and gravel quarry but in the year 2000 the Yorkshire Wildlife Trust bought it. The next three and a half years were spent in creating a mixed wetland of dykes, meres, lakes and shallow-water areas to provide habitats for a wide range of breeding and wintering birds including avocets, sandmartins, lapwings and redshanks. Since it opened in 2004 the North Cave Wetlands have become a shining example of how an industrial landscape can be transformed for the benefit of wildlife and is now a reserve of regional and national significance for bird watchers. One of these is Les Fisher from Hull and he summarised the appeal of this amenity in the following way:

The North Cave Wetlands consist of six lakes and opened in 2004. The area has been turned into a birdwatchers paradise.

Appleton Lane in North Cave. In the distance is the Londis store, the village shop, on Church Street. This was originally a single storey cottage to which an upper storey was added. Formerly it was a pork butcher's shop.

"The Wetlands are superb for bird watchers throughout the year with species ranging from the Green Woodpecker to the Avocet. The different habitats ensure that a wide variety of species will be seen and anything can turn up. The excellent hides provide enthusiasts with an ideal opportunity to observe birds at close hand."

The North Cave Wetlands are just one example of the tremendous community spirit that makes the village such a positive place to live for the whole project grew out of a campaign to prevent the redundant quarry becoming a landfill site. By bringing in visitors from far away the 'wetlands' have also benefited North Cave itself.

CHAPTER 20

SKIRLAUGH

Dissected by the busy A615 road the village of Skirlaugh, eight miles from Beverley, has seen a rapid growth in the last forty years. Much new house building has helped to swell the population of a village that in 1961 had only 522 people living there. In bygone times it was the Lambwath Stream that divided this ancient community for there were once two villages here: North Skirlaugh and South Skirlaugh.

Anyone unfamiliar with the pronunciation of East Riding place names might be forgiven for thinking that with 'laugh' as part of its name Skirlaugh was some kind of 'comic creation'. However the true origins of this unusual name remain controversial. In the Domesday Book of 1086 the village was called 'Schireslai', said to be derived from 'divide' or 'cut' and thought to refer to the Lambwath Stream which separated North Skirlaugh from South Skirlaugh. However, another authority on the village suggests that the name Skirlaugh came from 'bright clearing' and originated with the Angles and later Scandinavian invaders.

During the Middle Ages this ancient community was called 'Skirlaw' and the name became famous because of its associations with one of the area's most celebrated sons: Walter Skirlaw. He was born in Skirlaugh which was then part of the parish of Swine, around 1330 but very little is known of his family circumstances. However it is claimed that Walter Skirlaw must have born into a fairly prosperous family since his sister Joan became prioress of Swine, an important East Riding religious house in the Middle Ages. Whatever the truth of this it is clear that Walter Skirlaw was a very talented individual who chose the church as his career at a time when the influence of churchmen in affairs of state was often considerable.

The late fourteenth century was a period when the Black Death was decimating the population of Europe and with declining numbers of clergy Skirlaw's abilities seem to have marked him out for rapid advancement. With his training in the law he was chosen, around 1356, to be the registrar of John Thoresby, the Archbishop of York who three years later began sending him on diplomatic missions to the Pope's court in Avignon. Skirlaw's abilities as an international negotiator were recognised by his appointment to the court of King Edward the Third (1376) and soon after he was involved in negotiations with both the

St Augustine's Church in the village dates from the late fourteenth century and was built with funds provided by Skirlaugh-born Walter Skirlaw, the Bishop of Durham. It has been described as a "gem of the early perpendicular style."

Walter Skirlaw was a figure of national importance in the Middle Ages and he acted as a foreign diplomat during the reigns of Edward the Third, Richard the Second and Henry the Fourth. As Bishop of Durham (1388-1406) he made a large contribution to the funding of the central tower of York Minster and of the Great East Window. In this image he appears as the kneeling figure at the base of the window.

French and the Scots. At a turbulent and dangerous time in English history Skirlaw was above all a survivor, living into his seventies. Skirlaw's survival skills and his abilities were such that he served both Richard the Second and the man who overthrew him Henry Bolingbroke (King Henry the Fourth). In 1388 he became Bishop of Durham and effectively the ruler of the surrounding area, known as the County Palatine of Durham. In this role Skirlaw wielded both great power and great patronage and in many ways he was independent of royal control. His huge personal wealth was also put to good use in supporting a number of good causes like building bridges and contributing to the cost of work on York Minster, Durham Cathedral and Howden Minster.

Skirlaw was also generous to his home village for before his death in 1406 he had paid for a new church which was dedicated to St Augustine. This church has long been regarded as the best example of early perpendicular architecture in England. Succeeding generations left the church largely intact and this together with restoration work in the nineteenth and twentieth centuries, including the re-pointing of the stonework by local volunteer Edward Brown in the 1980's and 1990's, means that the residents of Skirlaugh have an historic gem at the heart of their village. A visit to see this masterpiece of late medieval church architecture is to be recommended.

Another of Skirlaugh's oldest buildings stands alongside the main road at the northern edge of the village and these day's houses library and educational departments of the East Riding County Council. However when it was built in 1838-1839 its purpose was far different. Designed by John and William Atkinson of York the building was originally a workhouse built to house the various classes of paupers of the forty-two parishes in the Skirlaugh Poor Law Union. Under the New Poor Law of 1834 accommodation in a well-regulated workhouse became the preferred way of dealing with poor people who sought help 'from the parish'. To deter only the most desperate from applying, and to keep down the cost of poor relief, life under the workhouse regime was made deliberately hard and unpleasant with strict regulations, a meagre diet and hard monotonous work the order of the day. The layout of the workhouse was designed to segregate the sexes for at Skirlaugh a central courtyard was divided by a partition to separate males and females.

The operations of the Skirlaugh Poor Law Union were overseen by forty-two guardians elected to represent the interests of the constituent parishes (like Long Riston, Hornsea and Brandsburton). The East Riding Archive in Beverley now holds the surviving records of the Union and a directory of 1892 tells us that the Guardians met every alternate Friday in the boardroom of the workhouse. Since poor relief was paid for by a tax (the poor rate) on local property owners it is not surprising that they were well represented on the Board of Guardians and, for example, in 1892 the

The workhouse in Skirlaugh was built in 1838-1839 to serve parishes in mid-Holderness. Closed during the First World War it later became the headquarters of Holderness Borough Council and is now used by East Riding County Council.

chairman was William Bethell of Rise-Park, a substantial landowner in this area of Holderness.

An almost miserly concern of the guardians to save money was shown by a letter, dated 3rd March 1888, from the Skirlaugh clerk to his counterpart at the Scarborough workhouse. The letter concerned a destitute and pregnant twenty-six year old woman from Scarborough who had turned up at the Skirlaugh workhouse on the 5th February and had been admitted "as she was evidently near her confinement." The letter asked for reimbursement of the cost of looking after the woman and her child since Skirlaugh was "not her place of settlement and the burden of the woman's maintenance has been improperly and illegally thrown on this Union"

Census returns for the late nineteenth century are particularly useful in showing us who was living at the workhouse, their former occupation and where they came from. The 1881 census reveals that the

144

This post-mill was in use on Beningholme Lane in Skirlaugh until around 1910. It was demolished in 1944. (Image courtesy of the East Riding Museums Service)

workhouse was being run by Robert Catlin and his wife Mary and in their charge were seventy-six residents ranging from a one-year-old boy (Alfred Johnson) to an eighty seven year old widower (Isaiah Armstrong). Of these residents only nine had been actually born in Skirlaugh itself.

It is also possible to deduce something of the circumstances that had brought these unfortunate people to the workhouse. One of the categories of inmates were orphans too young to take care of themselves and from the 1881 census we learn of the presence of Fanny Dearing, age twelve, born at nearby Ellerby, her sister Mary, age nine, together with her two brothers Alfred, age eleven and Herbert, age six.

In the blunt language of the nineteenth century some inmates of the workhouse were described as 'imbeciles' while others, considered to be 'lunatics', were sometimes transferred to the East Riding Lunatic Asylum near Walkington. One of these was Thomas Roger, age sixty-seven, described in the asylum records as "a restless demented old man." He was transferred from the Skirlaugh workhouse to the Walkington asylum on the 13th February 1875 but was dead of "senile debility" only six weeks later. Another of Skirlaugh's workhouse inmates who made the journey to the Walkington asylum was Sarah Dunn, age twenty-eight, who was said to suffer from delusions and was described in a report as "a small girl rather reduced in bodily health and condition and incapable of using her legs because of paralysis." Comments on her condition span the period from her arrival at the asylum in January 1873 to her death in February 1887 when it was reported, "her condition is almost skin and bone."

The Skirlaugh institution had a relatively short life with the children being transferred to the Beverley Workhouse in 1915 and the other inmates a year later. It was then used as a military hospital and for housing before the redundant buildings became the headquarters of the Holderness Borough Council.

Another old building that has been adapted to a new purpose is the National School on Benningholme Lane, built in 1860 at a cost of £919 including the land. In 1968 a new school was provided nearby and so the original one became the village hall. Thanks to the hard work of the Village Hall Committee the building has undergone a major refurbishment and reopened in July 2009 as part of the Skirlaugh Gala celebrations.

Skirlaugh has grown quickly in the last forty years because many people saw the advantages of the village as a place to commute to work in Hull or Beverley. From the 1960s, for example, the Cawood Estate was

This busy junction close to the Duke of York public house lies at the heart of the village. In a directory of 1823 John Stabler was the licensee of the Duke of York.

built bringing an influx of new families many of who are now enthusiastic supporters of community activities. One of these activities is the production of an impressive monthly newsletter by a dedicated team of enthusiasts keeping everyone informed about forthcoming events in the village.

CHAPTER 21

NORTH FERRIBY

The rise of private motoring since the Second World War has led to the rapid growth of many East Riding villages and none more so than North Ferriby, eight miles west of Hull. However an influx of newcomers is nothing new to this ancient community for in the late eighteenth century the village high street saw the building of fine mansions by merchants from Hull eager to experience country living at its best.

Of all the villages in the East Riding the process of change and expansion came earlier to North Ferriby than elsewhere because of the advantages of its location. As John Tickell, writing in the 1790s, said of the place:

> "Ferriby is a very pleasant village, delightfully situated in the most elevated and healthy part of the county and full of handsome buildings belonging to several wealthy merchants of Hull."

North Ferriby was different in other ways too since evidence indicates a history dating back three thousand five hundred years. In 1937 two local men, Ted and Clauude Wright discovered the first of three ancient plank built boats on Ferriby foreshore. Radio carbon dating showed that these craft were built around 2000BC, in the Bronze Age, and makes the Ferriby boats the earliest known boats found in Europe.

The location of this ancient settlement so close to the River Humber also meant that North Ferriby was also influenced by invasions of the British Isles at later times. The name of the village indicates the influence of Danish settlers of the ninth century for 'Ferja-by' means the 'place of the ferry' and a charter granted by King Canute around the year 1035 was meant to safeguard this important crossing over the Humber to South Ferriby.

The continuing significance of North Ferriby during the Middle Ages is indicated by the establishment of a small priory there in around 1150, by Lord Eustace Broomfleet de Vesci. The monks would have provided hospitality for pilgrims en route from the ferry to the shrine of St John at Beverley and where 'miraculous cures' were supposedly brought about. One such miracle happened, it was said, in 1321 when John, the ten-year old son of William of Ferriby, was struck dumb by 'the

The half-scale reconstruction of the Ferriby Boat 'Oakleef', sails past the shoreline where it was found. Courtesy of 'The Ferriby Heritage Trust'.

mysterious judgement of God.' According to the evidence the boy was 'cured' after a blessing by the prior of North Ferriby and a visit to the shrine of St John at Beverley. This small priory of six canons (believed to have been in the New Walk area of the village) existed for four hundred years but was dissolved in 1536 during the reign of King Henry the Eighth. All traces of the priory disappeared soon after the dissolution.

Until fresh air and country living became the fashion of Hull's elite in the eighteenth century North Ferriby would have remained a small quiet place, bounded by High Street and Low Street and dominated by the needs of farming. Much remains in High Street to remind us of the changes wrought by men like Sir Henry Etherington (1731-1819) the man responsible for Ferriby House which was built around 1785 and is now a nursing home.

Across the road stands another example of Georgian good taste: Ferriby Hall (now Medici's Restaurant). The arrival of the railway in North Ferriby in 1840 meant that for those who could afford it commuting by train into Hull which was only fifteen minutes away, was now a possibility. A local directory and the 1891 census shows the presence in the village of John Ostler, a corn merchant of the firm of

Post Office and Telephone Exchange, Ferriby.

Old postcard showing North Ferriby around 1900.

The Georgian elegance of Ferriby Hall, now Medici's Restaurant.

Kuypers, Ostler and Scott, who lived at Ferriby Hall with his wife Margaret and two sons. At a time when the well-to-do commonly employed domestic servants Ferriby Hall was also home to a parlour maid, a cook a housemaid and a kitchen maid.

Local people benefited not only from the employment opportunities provided by these grand houses but also from the generosity of their owners. By 1844 the Turner family lived at Ferriby House and became substantial landowners in the village. In 1878 the Turners built a new school for the village children and provided some money for its day-to-day expenses. This Church of England School, from 1902, became the responsibility of East Riding County Council and in the 1920s and 1930s was visited regularly by the County Inspector.

A directory of 1892 listed John Hornby as the schoolmaster and he was still there in January 1922 when the inspector wrote:

> "Mr Hornby is still vigorous for his age (61) but is retiring at the end of March. His successor will find the school in a fair state. The bulk of the pupils come from good homes and afford material for good results."

North Ferriby United in a pre-season friendly against Hull City.

However, the new headmaster, William Frankish, was soon the victim of a smear campaign for reasons unconnected with education. There were allegations that he was neglecting the school but the inspector dismissed these when he wrote in January 1925:

"These rumours should be received with much caution. Mr Frankish, much against his will, is acting as secretary to the local branch of the British Legion. In an effort to run the club on proper lines he has offended one or two delinquents. These people have made efforts to say damaging things about Mr Frankish."

It would seem that these difficulties must have resolved themselves for Mr Frankish continued in post for another ten years despite the problems created by overcrowded inadequate buildings. In July 1932, for example, the inspector reported that one hundred and thirty three pupils were being taught in a room separated only by a partition and that "teachers are usually talking against each other."

In February 1938 North Ferriby School had one hundred and fifty seven pupils on roll whereas thirty years later there were four hundred and seventy three. This increase in numbers reflected the growing popularity of the village in the post-war years with much new house building like the Riverview Estate and the Parkfield Estate which filled up the space between the High Street and the new Ferriby by-pass which opened in 1961.

With the increasing numbers has come a growing community spirit. One of the village success stories has been North Ferriby United Football Club formed in 1934 as a result of a village meeting. Since the Second World War the club has gone from strength to strength with considerable investment being made in new facilities at their ground off Church Road.

A more recent innovation is the 'North Ferriby Open Gardens Event' held in June each year. The village has a number of keen gardeners and this fund-raising event gives an opportunity of villagers and visitors to see the results of their labours. The event began about six years ago as a way of raising money for North Ferriby Primary School and in 2008 generated about £3000 for PTA funds.

North Ferriby is also famous for its connections with the acclaimed local artist Tom Harland whose studio and gallery at Low Street in the village first opened in 1981. Tom is one of the best-known artists currently working in the East Riding and many of his watercolours adorn the walls of important local companies like BP, Ideal Standard and Reckitt Benckiser. Tom developed his skills at Hull Regional College of Art from 1961 to 1966 before briefly becoming a teacher. Since 1970 he has been working full time as an artist initially employed by advertising agencies and by architects in producing 'artists impressions' of new building projects. When asked about how North Ferriby had influenced his work he replied:

> "The Humber Estuary has been my inspiration and I walk along the shoreline every day to observe the sky and the clouds and to see light reflected back from the river."

When the journalist Edward Baines visited North Ferriby in 1823 it had a population of just three hundred and forty seven people. Almost two centuries later that population now stands at about three thousand six hundred. Yet although the village has grown it has retained a tremendous

153

The artist Tom Harland was born in North Ferriby and has completed commissions for many of East Yorkshire's famous companies like BP and Ideal Standard. (Image courtesy of Tom Harland)

sense of identity and community and the list of village organisations is remarkable in both its scope and in demonstrating involvement across all ages and all interests.

CHAPTER 22

WETWANG

For those people who are unfamiliar with East Yorkshire the name 'Wetwang' which is five miles north-west of Driffield, is often a source of great amusement. However such is the unique nature of the name that fiction writers like J.R.R.Tolkien and Douglas Adams have used it as a location for their stories.

The origins of Wetwang are controversial. Some maintain that the name comes from the Anglian words 'wet-wang' meaning 'wet field' while others suggest it is derived from the Norse word 'Vettvangr' meaning 'field for the trial of a legal action.' Yet although Wetwang may have been an important centre of justice in Viking times its beginnings were even older for the area is rich in prehistoric earthworks especially the dry valley north of the village (Wetwang Slack). Of particular interest was the discovery, from 1984, of three Iron Age chariot burials. In the first excavation was a young man with his chariot, sword and shield, in the second, dating from about 100 BC, was a woman, her chariot and her personal possessions including a mirror and in the third another man with his sword and other weapons. In March 2001 at the eastern end of the village came another remarkable discovery. During the building of a small housing development a fourth chariot burial was found and excavated by a team of archaeologists. In the grave they found the skeleton of a woman in a crouched position together with her mirror and with pig joints covering her upper body. The dismantled pieces of her chariot had been placed around and over her body and the grave filled in. The burial of personal possessions and food suggest something about Celtic beliefs in the afterlife but also indicate that the occupant of the grave was a person of wealth and importance. These and other discoveries at Wetwang suggest that this was a farming community growing corn and other crops and keeping cattle, sheep and pigs long before the Roman occupation of Britain.

Like much of the East Riding Wetwang remained largely an agrarian community until recent times and in 1823 the journalist Edward Baines said of the place and its 422 inhabitants:

"This village is principally occupied by farmers and their labourers."

155

The skeleton of a woman found during the excavation of an iron-age chariot burial (2001). (Image courtesy of the East Riding Museums Service)

There were seventeen farms in Wetwang in 1851 and by looking at village directories and census records it is possible to put a human face on village life of that time. In the 1881 census for example there is an entry for the household of Leonard Thompson a forty-seven year old farmer of two hundred acres who lived on Front Street. Also living there was his wife, four male farm servants and one female general servant. At the other end of the social spectrum but also living on Front Street was William Barrett a forty-year old agricultural labourer, his wife Jane and their six daughters.

In the late nineteenth century farming was still labour-intensive but the growing use of machinery sometimes led to accidents. From a local newspaper of 23rd June 1883 we learn of a fatal mishap at Wetwang to an agricultural labourer, Francis Rookes. His hand was severed by a straw-cutting machine and despite being treated by a local doctor and rushed to Hull Infirmary he died soon afterwards.

The development of railways in East Yorkshire during the 19th century at least meant that isolated rural communities like Wetwang now had access to improved medical services in Driffield and Hull. Wetwang got its own station with the opening of the Malton to Driffield Railway in

The railway station at Wetwang in the days of the North Eastern Railway. The station was the busiest village station on the Malton to Driffield line in the early 20th century. The station opened in 1853. It closed to passengers in 1950 and to goods traffic in 1958.

Wetwang's famous 'mere' was once the home to black swans.

1853 but newspaper reports of the time show that local inhabitants could cause trouble to railway employees. On the 20th January 1877 a drunken local builder called John Roe seeking to travel from Wetwang to Driffield became involved in an argument with the stationmaster. He was subsequently charged with being drunk, disorderly and using abusive language and was fined £1 plus costs.

Wetwang's farming legacy is very much a part of the village of today with a mix of Georgian and Victorian farmhouses and workers cottages still much in evidence. At the heart of the village is the large mere or pond (probably a natural one formed by glacial action in the Ice Age) and which once provided the water supply for this ancient community. Another of Wetwang's oldest surviving features is the Church of St Nicholas the tower of which dates from the 12th century while other parts were built in the 15th century. According to a 19th century history of the village the church underwent a thorough restoration in 1845 at a cost of £1,500 with some of the money provided by Sir Tatton Sykes, the main landowner and benefactor in the village. He also

Following the death of Richard Whiteley in 2005 the BBC weather forecaster Paul Hudson was elected 'Mayor of Wetwang'. (Image courtesy of Paul Hudson)

paid for the building of a school on Pulham Lane in 1843 and this still forms part of today's Wetwang Primary School.

A walk around the village today can also provide numerous clues to its past including road names like 'Joiner's Lane', house names like 'Tailor's Cottage' and businesses like 'Old Smithy Holiday Cottage.' A local directory of 1892 helps us to understand where these names came from for in that year the village had two blacksmiths (William Agar and Charles Buttle), a tailor (William Blowman) and a joiner/wheelwright (William Ewbank). As late as 1937 Wetwang still had a diverse range of trades including five shopkeepers, a saddler, a shoemaker and a blacksmith. Although these have now disappeared the village pubs from earlier times remain together with one of the finest fish and chip shops in East Yorkshire: 'Harpers'. This occupies the site of Wetwang's old fire station and when it first opened was aptly named 'The Old Fire Plaice'!

One of its regular customers was renowned television personality Richard Whiteley (1943-2005) for free fish and chips was one of the 'perks' of his role as 'Honorary Mayor of Wetwang.' Richard Whiteley became 'mayor' in 1998 when he was invited to do so by the folk of the village after joking about the name 'Wetwang' on his Channel Four quiz show 'Countdown'. In fact the tradition of electing a so-called 'mayor' dates back to the 1920s when it was part of Wetwang's 'village fair' events to raise money for the village hall. It was therefore apt that when the new Community Hall was built it was Richard Whiteley who performed the opening ceremony in 2000.

One of the aims of having a 'mayor' is to put Wetwang on the map and generate publicity for the village and so when it came to choosing a successor to Richard in 2006 it is not surprising that the villagers selected BBC 'Look North' weatherman Paul Hudson. Paul beat off competition from other celebrities by polling 44% of the 152 votes cast. One of his first duties as 'mayor' was to unveil a plaque in June 2006 in memory of his predecessor and he also attends other village events like the school fete and judges the Wetwang 'Scarecrow Festival' which is held in May each year. Sharp-eyed viewers of the BBC 'Look North' programme will also have noticed how frequently 'Wetwang' appears on the weather map when Paul is the forecaster!

By the time of the 2001 Census the population of Wetwang parish had risen to 672 and in common with many East Riding villages the period since the Second World War has seen much new house building . An analysis of population figures show that numbers in the village rose by 66% between 1971 and 1991 showing the enormous appeal of this lovely Wolds community.

160

CHAPTER 23

SUTTON-UPON-DERWENT

One of the great joys of summer motoring trips is diverting away from the major trunk roads and exploring the quieter by-ways of East Yorkshire. Those who head to York along the busy A1079 road from Market Weighton may have noticed signs to 'Sutton upon Derwent' and for those who enjoy getting 'off the beaten track' this is a village well worth seeing.

Although the name 'Sutton' is Anglo-Saxon in origin, meaning south-farm, there is evidence that the Romans were here too. Archaeological investigations in 1991 close to Sutton Hall revealed evidence of Roman pottery, bricks and tiles and it seems likely that the presence of nearby Eboracum (Roman York) meant that the origin of the village was as a crossing place on the River Derwent.

In the Middle Ages 'Sutton' on the east bank and Elvington on the west probably developed as a result of their position near to the river. A ferry was recorded as early as 1368 but by the end of the fourteenth century had been replaced by a bridge. The meadows close to Sutton's old twin-arch bridge were often affected by flooding and in the eighteenth century the road leading to it had to be raised on an embankment to overcome this problem. Similarly, two of Sutton's oldest surviving buildings: the Church of St Michael, which dates from the 12th century and the nearby 18th Manor House were built on an elevated position above the level of the Derwent flood plain. These days there are moorings close to the bridge for pleasure craft but in earlier times the river was used for boats transporting coal, timber and other goods, for salmon fishing and to power a water mill. Following a fire 'Sutton Mill' was rebuilt in 1826-1827 and had two water wheels and seven pairs of stones to grind corn into flour. The 1851 Census shows the presence of Joseph Hatfield a corn miller and seeds man and records that he was employing eight men. Living at the mill with him were his brother William Hatfield who was the foreman miller, his bookkeeper Robert Wright, his carter Christoper Swales and two domestic servants.

A corn mill was a vital facility in a rural village where the main occupation was agriculture and a directory of 1823 records the names of eight farmers and they would have employed many others to carry out the labour-intensive work of the time. Typical of the mid 19th century was

An old picture postcard of Sutton-upon-Derwent from around 1900.

William Beal of Sutton Farm who in 1851 was farming three hundred and thirty acres and employing eight men. Like Sutton Mill many of these workers 'lived in' and the 1851 Census shows that William Beal's household consisted of eight people including five 'farm servants.'

By law, parishes like Sutton-upon-Derwent had to make provision for those who because of factors like old age, ill health, bereavement or unemployment could not support themselves. Under the 1834 Poor Law accommodation in a well-regulated workhouse became the preferred way of dealing with paupers but some parishes continued to give financial support to those living in their own homes. One of these was Sutton resident Elizabeth Smith who in the 1851 Census was described as a twenty-seven year old pauper. Living with her were her daughters Mary aged nine and Ann aged two.

From 1834 Sutton-upon-Derwent had been made part of the Pocklington Poor Law Union and the officials responsible for helping the poor were vigilant in 'chasing' absent fathers to make them pay for their offspring. From records held at the East Riding Archive in Beverley we know that on the 23rd April 1842 the Pocklington Guardians had applied to a magistrate for "an order against Joseph Falkingham to compel him to support Elizabeth Smith's bastard child chargeable to the parish of Sutton upon Derwent."

The cost of poor relief fell on the ratepayers of Sutton-upon-Derwent and in 1842 records show that they were paying about £120 a year as their share of the expenses of the Pocklington Poor Law Union. These costs later included the operation of a new workhouse opened at Pocklington in 1852. The destitute turning up at the workhouse to seek assistance, despite the poor diet and the harsh discipline it offered, included Sutton upon Derwent resident George Mitchell. The workhouse 'admissions and discharge' book shows that on the 27th December 1852 he was admitted, endured the humiliation of having the number '4' affixed to his clothes and was discharged "upon his own notice" on the 4th March 1853.

Periods of temporary unemployment or ill health meant that the poor and their families had little alternative when seeking help other than presenting themselves at the workhouse. One of these was Benjamin Lister from Sutton upon Derwent, a forty-five year old platelayer for the North Eastern Railway. At the time of the 1871 Census he, his wife and their four children were all resident in the Pocklington Workhouse. More tragic was the case of Emily Booth a seventy-four year old widow from the village who died after being taken to the workhouse in December

The single lane twin-arch bridge crosses the River Derwent.

1893. According to the evidence presented at her inquest she had lived alone on parish relief of three shillings per week after the death of her husband but had become addicted to laudanum, an opium based drug popular in Victorian times for a variety of ailments. According to villagers who knew this unfortunate woman she had "sold everything that was given to her to obtain supplies of laudanum."

A directory of 1892 shows that Sutton upon Derwent had a variety of trades common among villages of the time and these included James Coultas (blacksmith), William Johnson (shoemaker), Walter Midgely (tailor and postmaster) and Thomas Throssel (joiner, wheelwright and agricultural implement maker). The directory also lists Thomas Bootland the licensee of the 'St Vincent Arms' Public House and he also brewed beer here. Earlier in the nineteenth century this famous Sutton pub had been called the 'Clarges Arms' after Sir Thomas Clarges who became Lord of the Manor in 1731. The change of pub name came about when in 1857 the manor passed to Carnegie Jervis, 3rd Viscount St Vincent. Those who have studied the pub sign of the St Vincent Arms will have seen a painting of a naval battle and this represents the 1797 Battle of Cape St

The victorious Woodhouse Grange cricket team with Captain Steve Burdett holding the National Village Cup at Lords in 2007. (Image courtesy of the MCC)

Vincent when the British commander John Jervis defeated a much larger Spanish force in Portuguese waters.

These days the 'St Vincent Arms' and their suppliers Fullers Brewery, are the proud sponsors of another of Sutton's claims to fame: its well-known and highly successful village cricket team. The Woodhouse Grange Cricket Club has an impressive ground in open countryside on Sandhill Lane about two miles from the village. The club was established in 1942 by Thomas Hobson, a veteran batsman, who began farming at Woodhouse Grange Farm which is part of the Crown's Derwent Estate in the nineteen thirties. From its beginnings as a cricket club for workers on the estate Woodhouse Grange has grown to be a club for all abilities and age groups. Their accomplished 'First Eleven' won the 'Npower Village Cup' at Lords in both 1995 and 2007 and were the runners up in 2008. For over fifty years Woodhouse Grange Cricket Club has also been the most successful club in the York Senior League and were league champions in 2008 and 2009. From its beginnings under Tom Hobson the club has seen that the way forward is to promote cricket to youngsters and the development of its Junior Section has long been seen as a priority.

Sutton upon Derwent's thriving community spirit is helped by its imposing village hall built in 1929-31 as a result of a gift by a local well-wisher and is rated as one of the best of its type in Yorkshire. These days the hall is home to activities like badminton, indoor bowls, keep fit, early music and a pre-school club. In addition the village hosts a number of

The Village Hall is an important community asset. According to a plaque the building was "erected 1929-31 by the Reverend M.H. Pimm and Parishioners, the result of a gift".

annual events like Bonfire Night fireworks, a Christmas Carols evening with mulled wine and a summer fete.

Sutton upon Derwent is a village that has seen significant growth in the years since 1991 with new house building and some conversion of its older buildings to provide accommodation. Being only eight miles southeast of York the village has become a popular commuter settlement for those working in the city and also in Pocklington. In the last hundred years its population has fluctuated widely partly due to the changing fortunes of agriculture and falling to as low as two hundred and seventy people in 1931. However in the last twenty years, thanks to its growing popularity as a safe and desirable rural location, its new housing developments and its remarkable community spirit the population has grown rapidly to around six hundred people.

CHAPTER 24

ELLERKER

When people are asked about the 'magic ingredients' that make up a perfect English village they will often bring to mind a settlement of traditional cottages clustered around narrow lanes, a village green, a meandering beck of crystal clear water, a picturesque church and a sense of 'belonging' that a thriving community spirit encourages. Ellerker, ten miles west of Hull, has all these attributes although the downside to this image of a rural 'idyll' is that it no longer has a shop, a pub or a school. Yet this village of around three hundred people remains a very desirable place to live because of its good road communications via the A63 / M62 corridor and its location about two and a half miles from Brough Railway Station.

The name Ellerker is probably derived from the landscape of the ninth century encountered by the Scandinavian invaders who settled here. It is thought that the word comes from 'Alder Marsh' (alor kjarr) and evolved into 'Alrecher' by the eleventh century and 'Elreker' in the thirteenth. An important local family who lived here from the time of the Norman Conquest until around 1960 also used the name Ellerker. Like others in the village in medieval times they would have been engaged in farming, fishing in the nearby Humber and wildfowling on the surrounding carrs and marshes. One of the farmers listed in the 1766 enclosure award for Ellerker (when the open fields and commons disappeared to make way for compact farms) was William Ellerker and members of his family continued to farm there during the nineteenth century.

The landowners who benefited from this change to the rural landscape met the costs of enclosure and sometimes they had to borrow the money needed. From a letter of June 1769 held by the East Riding Archive we learn of allegations by Paul Woolas of Ellerker that his father had, in 1768, fled from the village to Hull with "another man's wife" and that he had earlier borrowed money to enclose his lands at Ellerker but was refusing to pay it back. Woolas was to claim: "he is spending his substance much faster than he got it and is likely to die in a state of beggary."

Although many of the landowners who owned estates at Ellerker were absentees (like Thomas Broadley of Ferriby) they and their tenants

George Mackley, corn and flour dealer and also miller of Ellerker, taken in 1910. (Image courtesy of the East Riding Museums Service)

Main Street at Ellerker on a summer's day.

were vital in the rural economy of the time. The influence of farming can be seen in the logbooks of Ellerker National School, built in 1845 at a cost of £300. On May 29th 1863 the schoolmaster wrote:

> "A very thin school. Many of the boys gone to weed the corn and the bigger girls are staying at home to help their mothers."

Three months later the teacher recorded that although the summer holidays were at an end he had opened the school on 21st August with only twenty-eight pupils present because the farmers had not succeeded in getting all their crops in "on account of the wet weather."

Although absenteeism to undertake farm work was often seen by Ellerker School as excusable more general truancy was not. An entry in the logbook dated February 5th 1886 records that the school attendance officer had obtained a summons against Thomas Donkin to appear at the Welton Police Office to answer for the bad attendance of his child. Three days later the logbook recorded that:

"The School Attendance Officer called to say Thomas Donkin had been fined two shillings and sixpence (12p)."

Despite the sanction of corporal punishment available to the teachers of the time the children from Ellerker and Brantingham who attended the school were as capable of 'high-spirits' as those of today and on November 19th 1920 the logbook recorded:

"A Police Constable called regarding damage to Mr Pickering's mangel-wurzel pie and to find the boy who threw a cup into a motorcar driven by the Superintendent of Police."

Early in 1921 a new headmistress, Harriet Churnside, arrived to take up her appointment and on the 15th March the East Riding Schools' Inspector, Mr J Moffat, made a visit to look at the work of the sixty-five children registered to attend. In view of subsequent events his assessment of the new head teacher makes interesting reading for even at this early stage he suggested that this rather formidable lady might be difficult to work with. Her two assistants, Miss Padley and Miss Miller, were soon to find that she had a fiery temper and was critical of their work. In the circumstances it is not surprising that the school logbook recorded that on the 31st August 1921:

"Miss Padley terminated her duties at this school today."

More bizarre events were to follow when Miss Churnside turned her temper and blunt language towards the second assistant teacher who objected to being bullied in that way. The inspector's report of 6th March 1922 recorded that:

"When spoken to by the Head Teacher Miss Miller had become insubordinate. Unfortunately Miss Miller lived with Miss Churnside and shared the only bed available."

According to the inspector the quarrel continued after school hours and into the night. Around 4.30am Miss Miller's nocturnal movements had woken the irascible Head Teacher from her slumbers on the far side of the bed. She had then reacted violently by propelling the unfortunate girl:

In 1844 the Reverend George Fyler Townesend wrote to the National Society of the Church of England to tell them that he intended to build a school for the children of Ellerker and Brantingham. This was finished in 1845 and opened in January 1846. The school building is now a private house.

"to her proper portion of the bed, perhaps a little beyond."

Being much offended the girl refused to get into bed again saying:

"I shall stay outside and so have a better case against you."

In the event the angry assistant decided to leave altogether and deserted her post at the school the following day. After listening to the Head Teacher's version of events Moffat wrote:

"I draw the following conclusions: Miss Churnside is a worker, a strict disciplinarian and expects her assistants to copy her example."

Having lost two teachers in such a brief period of time Harriet Churnside's stay at Ellerker was also short lived and she left in June 1922.

Her replacement was Mrs Gill. She too faced problems and in February 1924 the inspector wrote in his report:

> " She is not popular in the village. She does not appear to get on well with the vicar but I understand that he is a difficult man to deal with."

Two years later Moffat was back at Ellerker to investigate an allegation of assault by the Head Teacher against one of her pupils, Lawrence Walton. Gill denied having called the boy 'ugly' but did admit to hitting him on the shoulder with a ruler. Moffat wrote in his report of February 18th 1926:

> "I have tried to impress on Mrs Gill that she should avoid nagging her pupils and that she must administer corporal punishment rarely and in the proper manner."

In the years before the Second World War children left Ellerker School at the age of fourteen but with the raising of the school leaving, changes to school organisation and the building of South Hunsley Secondary School in 1951, those aged eleven and above transferred there. The numbers attending Ellerker School declined rapidly from the late 1950s and it closed in July 1967.

Other changes too were apparent in the years after 1945. One of the best-loved features of Ellerker is the beck that meanders through the village and this once powered a corn mill, where Mill House stands today. Today the waters of the beck are kept clean but this was not always the case and in 1897 a complaint was made to Beverley District Council about the 'stench' coming from it and asking for steps to be taken to clean it out. Drinking water was still obtained from the beck and from pumps around the village until piped water was laid on after 1946.

Much of this historic village was protected from 1974 by the creation of a conservation area and among the buildings designated are those of Ellerker's famous 'Black Horse Restaurant'. Originally a group of two-up and two-down cottages built over three hundred years ago they had became a public house in the nineteenth century; in a directory of 1872 Isaac Carr was named as the licensee of the Black Horse.

The Black Horse Restaurant at Ellerker was once the Black Horse Public House. In a directory of 1892 Isaac Carr was named as the 'victualer'.

In the 21st century Ellerker remains a vibrant local community. For those living there the quarterly 'Ellerker News' keeps everyone informed of what is happening while the village hall is home to a number of activities including a Christmas party, the annual Ellerker Show, the monthly Ellerker Cinema and meetings of the Yorkshire Countrywomens' Association.

In the last sixty years Ellerker has changed a great deal from the simple farming community it once was although the large numbers of greenhouses growing strawberries and salad crops show the continuing importance of agriculture to the local economy. However, like other places close to the busy A63 route Ellerker continues to attract those moving to the area thanks to its old world charm and its thriving community spirit.

CHAPTER 25

CHERRY BURTON

Like many East Riding villages in the years since 1945 the growth of Cherry Burton, three miles north-west of Beverley, owes a great deal to the rise of the motorcar for until comparatively recently the village consisted of just one main street and was a typical farming community. It was the building of new houses and bungalows in places like Canada Drive, the Meadows and Highcroft that led to a trebling of the population in just fifty years although the old village has been protected by the creation of a conservation area.

Anyone who has visited Cherry Burton will know what an attractive village it is with its eastern approach flanked by parkland and the high walled gardens of Cherry Burton Hall and Cherry Burton House. From the Church of St Michael the road then drops sharply to a dry valley where the bulk of the houses can be found along with the village pond, the modern school, a Costcutter Store, the village hall and the Bay Horse Public House.

The word 'Burh-tun' comes to us from the Angles, a Germanic tribe who settled in Eastern England from the fifth century AD, and means a fortified village or farmstead. To distinguish it from other 'Burtons' the name evolved into 'North Burton' by the thirteenth century and into 'Cherry Burton' by the fifteenth, probably because of the number of cherry trees growing in the area.

Although the present-day Church of St Michael only dates from the nineteenth century a church has stood on the site since at least the seventh century. One of Cherry Burton's claims to fame (or perhaps infamy) is that in 1530 the 'living' here was presented to one of Tudor England's most notorious clergymen, Edmund Bonner. Bonner was a powerful churchman during the reigns of both King Henry the Eighth and Mary Tudor and apart from Cherry Burton was rewarded with the 'livings' of a number of parishes scattered across the country including Blaydon in Durham and East Dereham in Norfolk. For pluralistic and absentee churchmen like Bonner the day-to-day care of souls in parishes like Cherry Burton would have been delegated to a lowly curate.

By 1539 Bonner was also Bishop of London and was to play an important part in the religious upheavals known as the Reformation. As a staunch Catholic Bonner became a fervent persecutor of Protestants

The Church of St Michael at Cherry Burton was rebuilt in 1852-1853 with interior restoration work in 1890.

A contemporary portrait of Edmund Bonner (1500-1569). The Canons of Beverley presented him to the Rectory of Cherry Burton in 1530.

during the bloodthirsty reign of Mary Tudor (1553-1558) and his cruelty in ordering floggings and executions to make his enemies recant their 'heresy' is legendary. Vilified in Protestant writings like Foxe's 'Book of Martyrs' he became known as 'Bloody Bonner' for ordering the burning of large numbers of English Protestants between 1555 and 1558. One of those 'heretics' was a weaver called Thomas Tomkins and it is said that Bonner had "forcibly shaved off his long evangelist's beard so he would look like a Catholic even if he wasn't one and had held his hand in a candle flame to give him a foretaste of what was in store for him if he failed to recant."

Summing up the intense hatred of Bonner felt by Protestants John Foxe said of him:

"This cannibal in three years space three hundred martyrs slew.
They were his food, he loved so blood, he spared none he knew."

In the centuries following these upheavals life in Cherry Burton would have been dominated by the needs of farming and the lives of the villagers by the occupants of the Manor House, which lay behind what is now 'The Bay Horse' Public House. In 1783 the manor was sold to David Burton Fowler and this began a long association between Cherry Burton and the Burton family that was to last until 1945.

It was David Burton Fowler who built Cherry Burton Hall on the site of an earlier house and successive members of the family continued to live at the hall, to own over a thousand acres of land around the village and to play an important part in the lives of the inhabitants. David Robinson Burton (1787-1854) was a Justice of the Peace and Deputy Lieutenant of the East Riding while his eldest son, David Burton (1820-1890), held the same positions and was also the first chairman of the East Riding County Council (1889). As JPs they were both important in the enforcement of the criminal law and in local administration. From a document held in the East Riding Archive for example, we know that David Robinson Burton was the JP who had Jane Hardbattle, a thirty five year old pauper from Cherry Burton, committed to the Beverley Workhouse in January 1830.

The Burtons as major landowners in Cherry Burton took their social responsibilities seriously and were important benefactors in the village. In 1894 a purpose built reading room with a library of two hundred books was opened by David Fowler Burton while the family also set aside four acres of parkland near their home as a village cricket ground. The Burtons also bought a disused Wesleyan Methodist Chapel on Main Street, enlarged it and turned into a village hall.

The 1881 census and directories of the same period are particularly useful in showing us both the importance of the Burton family and something of the lives of other villagers at that time. Living with David Burton at the Hall were four of his children, a governess and six servants including a cook, a footman, a gardener and a housemaid. Elsewhere in the village and at the other end of the social scale was George Gray, a thirty-seven year old agricultural labourer, his wife and their five children. However it would seem that Gray was in a position to better himself for by 1892 a directory of the village described him as a "reaping machine proprietor." Although agriculture was still labour-intensive there was increasing mechanisation on farms during the later nineteenth century. Sometimes this led to accidents and a local newspaper of 1874 tells us how Joseph Long of Cherry Burton was seriously injured in one such mishap. He was working a steam-powered machine used to chop horse fodder when his left hand was caught in the rollers. According to the newspaper:

> "his hand and arm to the elbow was chopped to pieces and the upper part of the arm much mangled. The limb had to be amputated near to the shoulder."

William Robson the last village blacksmith working at his forge near the village pond. (Image courtesy of Martin Peirson)

Even in the days of horse-drawn transport the people of Cherry Burton were able to benefit from its position near to Beverley and to use the Saturday market there. In June 1864 an inquest was held at the Bay Horse Public House into the death of George Pickering a fifty-four year old Cherry Burton farmer and cattle dealer who fell from his gig on the return journey from Beverley Market and subsequently died from his injuries.

A year later such a road journey would have been unnecessary since Cherry Burton was now connected to the rail network. The Market Weighton to Beverley section of the Hull to York line had opened in May 1865 and Cherry Burton Station with its platform, sidings, goods shed and coal drops lay about a mile from the village. A directory of 1882 tells us that George Coulson was then the stationmaster and he also acted as an agent for the 'Hand-in-Hand Insurance Society'.

However, by the 1950s increasing competition from road transport meant that ticket sales at Cherry Burton Station were in decline. The station closed to passengers in 1959 six years before the 'Beeching Axe' led to the closure of the line itself.

Despite the loss of its train service Cherry Burton remains a thriving village and its remarkable community spirit has been helped by an influx of newcomers. Two of the people who have made Cherry

The picturesque entrance to Cherry Burton. The road drops sharply to a dry valley where most of the village is located.

Burton their home are Rob and Rosemary Stanley who moved here from London in 1975.

In 2003 Rosemary became involved with the activities of a teenage group based at St Michael's Church who were keen to support the 'Fairtrade' movement. Concerned about those in poorer countries who were not able to earn enough money to feed their families or send their children to school they had begun selling fairtrade food, crafts and jewellery at a stall each Sunday morning. From these beginnings Rosemary and others encouraged the village to become involved in the national 'Fairtrade Fortnight'.

Such was the local enthusiasm for greater involvement that in July 2003 Cherry Burton became the East Riding's first 'Fairtrade Community' and only the second village in the country to be awarded the honour of being a 'Fairtrade Village.'

Another enthusiastic member of Cherry Burton's thriving community scene is Martin Peirson who married a local 'girl', Isabel Jackson, and has been here for twenty years. Isabel's family have lived in

The Doghouse Skiffle Group performing at a Cherry Burton Arts Night. (Image courtesy of Martin Peirson)

Cherry Burton for several generations and her great-grandfather was the last blacksmith in the village. With a keen interest in music Martin is now active in organising 'Cherry Burton Arts' evenings at the village hall. These events bring in a number of local and national musicians and bands for the entertainment of villagers and those further away.

With a population these days of around one and a half thousand people Cherry Burton itself is a hard act to follow among the villages of the East Riding. This thriving local community is as Martin Peirson says:

> "That classic combination of people that are prepared to do things and facilities to do them in! There is a church, a school, a pub, a village hall, sports facilities and pro-active set of people that like to use them – hence the many clubs and organisations."

CHAPTER 26

BRANTINGHAM

For keen walkers the stunning scenery of Brantingham Dale, twelve miles west of Hull, has long been a place of pilgrimage for it forms part of the Wolds Way. For those who are less energetic but enjoy exploring by car a descent of Dale Road, off the Raywell to South Cave road, is to be recommended too. The steeply sided and well-wooded valley of Brantingham Dale is also the picturesque setting for a village of great antiquity.

The scenic route along Dale Road soon brings you to All Saints Church, unusual in that this ancient place of worship lies some distance from the present-day village of Brantingham. The Anglo-Saxon name is thought to mean "the homestead of those dwelling in a steep place" and it is likely that the original Saxon settlement existed around the church and where the ancient Monk's Well would have provided the inhabitants with a plentiful supply of water. In fact the origins of Brantingham are much older and there is evidence of settlement here from the Stone Age while in 1994 a hoard of three thousand year old Bronze Age axe heads was found in an upland area near the village.

The Romans were here too as other archaeological discoveries have shown. About half a mile south east of the village, in a former stone quarry called 'Cockle Pits', two mosaic floors from a Romano-British farmhouse or villa were unearthed in 1941. Since this was the time of the Second World War the finds were recorded and then covered over again. When however in 1948 staff from Hull Museums returned to the site to remove them to a place of safety they found that one had been stolen. The disappearance of the 'First Geometric Mosaic' remains one of the greatest mysteries of archaeology and this important artefact has never been recovered. The 'Second Geometric Mosaic' was however transported to the Roman Gallery of the Hull and East Riding Museum in the High Street and remains as a testament to the skill of mosaic builders of the fourth century. The museum also contains other discoveries from the Brantingham Villa site for in 1962 another mosaic floor was unearthed (the Tyche Mosaic) together with some wall friezes.

The Anglo-Saxon settlers who gave Brantingham its name would have built their dwellings mostly of timber and thatch but in later centuries, for those who could afford it, Brantingham stone was also

A wall frieze from Brantingham Roman Villa (Image courtesy of the Hull and East Riding Museum)

available. In the 12th century the abbot of Meaux, near Wawne, acquired the quarry at Brantingham to supply the stone to build his abbey. After the dissolution of the monasteries King Henry VIII used that same stone to strengthen the defences of Hull.

In the centuries following the Norman Conquest of 1066 the lives of ordinary Brantingham folk would have been regulated by their Lord of the Manor and their daily routine by the needs of farming. By the sixteenth century these Lords of the Manor lived at Brantinghamthorpe Hall, two hundred feet above sea level and with magnificent views over the Humber estuary. Dating back to Elizabethan times the hall was

All Saints Church at Brantingham dates from the 12th century. The Church was practically rebuilt in 1872 (except for the tower) by Sir Christopher Sykes, the Lord of the Manor.

enlarged in the early nineteenth century and from the 1870s when it came into the possession of Sir Christopher Sykes (1831-1898).

He was the younger son of Sir Tatton Sykes of Sledmere and despite his wealth seems to have been a rather feeble individual who responded to his father's bullying by escaping to join the ranks of London society in the 1850s where he became a man of fashion and a connoisseur of books, china and furniture. Having left university without ever taking his degree Sykes was ultimately to become an MP for East Yorkshire but only made six speeches during his entire parliamentary career spanning twenty-four years.

Instead Sykes preferred to cultivate the friendship of royalty and joined the 'circle' of the Prince of Wales, the future Edward VII. Such was his 'slavish' devotion to his royal master that on numerous occasions he lavishly entertained the prince and his entourage at Brantinghamthorpe Hall. A document held by the East Riding Archive shows that in 1881 a total of 5686 people sat down for meals at the Hall.

Brantinghamthorpe and its gardens, rebuilt and beautified at great expense, became the base for weekend shooting parties and for Prince Edward to visit Doncaster Races with Sykes providing carriages to take his guests to the railway stations at either end of the journey. Such was his snobbery that he believed that Brantingham Church might not be good enough for his royal guests and so Sykes had it extensively rebuilt at a cost of £1,900. Unfortunately for him his regard for the Prince was not reciprocated for Edward subjected his 'courtier' to a number of indignities out of a sense of cruel fun. On one occasion the Prince poured a glass of brandy over his head at dinner to which Sykes responded, in his rather meek style: "As your majesty pleases."

Yet his adoration for the Prince of Wales was to prove his undoing for Sykes was driven to the verge of bankruptcy by it. A letter held by the East Riding Archive dated September 29th 1887 records:

"I have been talking to Christopher about his affairs and I grieve to find how miserable he is made by them and by the sad change in his whole manner of life which seems to impend."

In the end the disgrace of bankruptcy was only avoided through the generosity of his brother and the intervention of his sister-in-law who prevailed upon the Prince of Wales to pay off some of his more pressing debts.

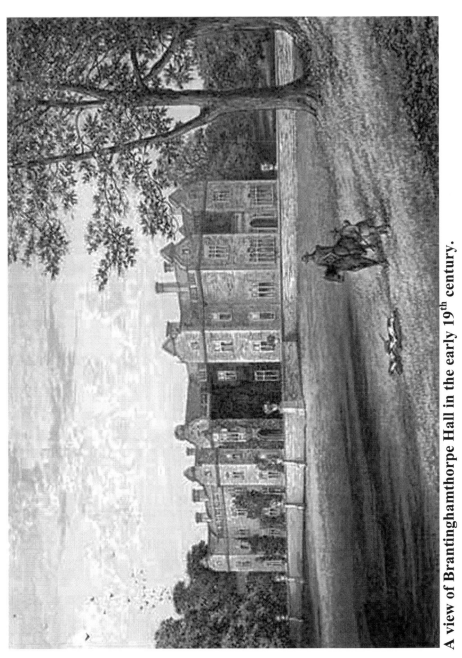

A view of Brantinghamthorpe Hall in the early 19th century.

Since Brantingham was an 'estate village' and effectively under the control of the Lord of the Manor it is not surprising that it made a major contribution to the income of Christopher Sykes. An account of his income in 1896 included Brantingham farm rents of £2053 and cottage rents of over £170. Census returns and local trade directories also give us some idea of how the needs of Christopher Sykes and his guests impacted on the village and its inhabitants. In 1879, for example, a trade directory of the village records the presence at 'Thorpe Cottage' of Robert Kingston, steward and gardener to Christopher Sykes, MP while the census of 1881 names Robert Himston (Gentleman Groom, Steward and Gardener), James Adcock (Foreman Gardener) and Albert Hammond (Coachman).

The 1881 Census also records the presence of Thomas Fleming described as a joiner, farmer and innkeeper, his wife Mary and daughter Frances. Fleming operated 'The Triton Inn' and the name reveals the influence that Sir Christopher Sykes had on the village for 'Triton' (a legendary Greek sea-god) was part of the Sykes coat of arms.

The public house dates back to the early eighteenth century and had been a coaching inn on the Hull to North Cave route where exhausted horses could be changed and weary travellers could obtain refreshment. Formerly known by other names like the 'Wounded Tiger' and the 'Half Moon' the pub was renamed 'The Triton' by its new owner Sir Christopher Sykes and has remained so ever since. The Triton Inn is reputedly haunted by the spirit of a lady in a long black dress tending the fire in the bar and the ghost of a young boy in an upstairs room!

In the 1970's with the increasing popularity of private motoring and 'eating out' the Triton was bought by the well known local grocery firm of William Jackson and Sons and it was they who extensively modernised it and changed it out of all recognition from the simple rural pub it had once been. The area in front of the Triton had once been an agricultural engineering business but this was now cleared to create a huge one hundred and twelve-space car park.

A major attraction of the Triton is its setting; the beautiful village of Brantingham has seen little change over the last hundred years and remains unspoilt by the large-scale development of new housing seen elsewhere. Although a number of cottages once occupied by estate workers have been sold in the years since the Second World War Brantingham is still essentially an estate village. The current owner of the estate is Charles Maxsted who lives at the heart of the village in Brantingham Hall, a Georgian Grade Two listed house. His grandfather

Brantingham's famous Triton Inn dates from the early 18th century and is famous for the quality of its cuisine.

bought the estate in 1929 and when he died in 1980 Charles Maxsted took over the house, the arable farm and the estate from him.

Brantingham's location at the foot of East Yorkshire's deepest dale makes it one of the loveliest places in the whole of the East Riding. It is a popular place among sightseers in the summer months while in wintertime its slopes see an influx of people with skis and toboggans.

CHAPTER 27

ETTON

While many places in the East Riding have seen a rapid expansion in the years since the Second World War the village of Etton, four miles northwest of Beverley, is an exception to the rule and its unspoilt charms help to explain the appeal of the place. Situated to the west of the busy B1248 Beverley to Malton road in its own picturesque dale, Etton today has a population of around two hundred and eighty-five people. When the journalist Edward Baines wrote about Etton in the 1820s there were three hundred and eighty people living there and like all East Riding villages of that time their lives would have been dominated by the needs of farming. Yet the nature of that agriculture had already begun to change.

One of Etton's most famous former residents was Thomas Carling, the founder of the famous Carling brewing empire. At the time of his birth in 1797 Etton would have looked quite different to how it appears today. Then there would have been a few scattered farmhouses and cottages together with three large open fields, with arable strips farmed communally and common grazing land to the west of the village. At the Easter Vestry meeting, village officials such as constables, pinders and waywardens were still appointed and the by-laws with their various fines confirmed:

> "None shall break the Stuble fields on the East side of West Wood with their Sheep before St John daye upon paine for every default – 3s 4d"

Thomas Carling's baptism record from Etton Church shows that his father, William Carling (1761-1844), was a farm labourer although by 1823 the directory of Edward Baines describes him as a 'farmer'. In those days East Riding villages like Etton were far more self-sufficient than they are today. That same 1823 directory lists a number of trades to serve local needs at a time when rural transport was still slow and difficult. These trades included a boot and shoemaker, a tailor, a corn miller and two shopkeepers. The production of beer was also very much a cottage industry and we know that William Carling brewed his own.

In the early nineteenth century Etton, like many other English villages, was undergoing profound changes. In order to improve farming

A harvest scene at Etton Fields Farm in 1916. (Image courtesy of the East Riding Museums Service)

A nineteenth century photograph of Thomas Carling of Etton, East Yorkshire and London Township, Ontario, Canada.

efficiency the scattered strips were being gathered together in enclosed farms. The Etton Enclosure Act was passed in 1818 and this may explain William Carling's change of status from farm labourer to farmer. It may also help to explain why, in 1818, his twenty-year old son, Thomas, (the youngest of William's five children) decided to leave Etton and seek his fortune in Canada.

The nineteenth century was a time when many working-class people, seeking a better life and the chance to own land of their own, left for the colonies. Without a single friend or acquaintance aboard the ship, Thomas Carling sailed from Hull on May 17th 1818. Arriving in Quebec a month later he then began an arduous journey on foot and by boat to London Township in Ontario where he obtained rights to one hundred acres of land. By the end of 1819 Carling was clearing trees to create farmland, building a log cabin and within a year had married the daughter of another pioneering family: Margaret Routledge. They brought up five children together in an area of Canada that was still largely wilderness.

After twenty years of enduring the hardships of Ontario farm life Thomas Carling sold his land and moved his family to the nearby settlement of London Township. Looking for something new to occupy his time his thoughts turned, in 1839, to the home-brewed beer that his father had made back in East Yorkshire. It was now that fate came to his aid. There was a large British garrison stationed in London Township and its troops were entitled to six pints of beer a day. Impressed by the quality of Carling's Yorkshire-inspired beer the officers and men persuaded him to start brewing it commercially in 1840.

Under the stewardship of Thomas Carling's sons the business continued to prosper and in 1878 they moved to a new, purpose-built brewery costing a quarter of a million dollars. By 1890 their workforce of one hundred men were turning out over thirty thousand barrels of ale, porter and lager each year. Later on new products were developed, for example, 'Carling Black Label' was first brewed in Canada in 1926 and the Carling brand went on to become famous throughout the world during the later twentieth century. Thanks to Thomas Carling's skill, enterprise and pioneering spirit in Canada the brewing business he established is today a global brand and is made by many different brewers around the world.

Meanwhile his father William Carling continued to live and farm at Etton until his death at the age of eighty-three and both he and his wife Margaret (1763-1838) were buried in the village churchyard. The continuing importance of farming to this rural community is indicated by the logbooks of Etton's Church of England School, which was built 1856 and are now held by the East Riding Archive Service in Beverley. At a time when children were often needed to do farm work their absences from school were often 'explained away' by the schoolmaster. In 1863 there were sixty-two children on roll and on July 1st he wrote:

> "Thirty three children present. Seven children are away pulling ketlocks from wheat while two are singling turnips. Several are going about the lanes with babies while their mothers are hoeing turnips."

In a small church school like Etton the role of the Rector was usually paramount and in a directory of 1882 the Reverend William Vernon was named as the clergyman. His importance to the school was reflected by a logbook entry of 10th February 1888 that recorded his death and which said "he had been in failing health for some time but that the end was sudden and unexpected."

More bizarre was an entry of the 17th February 1888 that reveals the very different attitudes to death in the nineteenth century from the present day. This said:

"Took the school children up to the Rectory at 1.15pm to see the body of the Rector – some seemed very affected."

More tragedy was soon to follow in April 1888 when an auction of the late clergyman's effects took place at Etton Rectory. Around fifty people had crowded into an upstairs room for the afternoon sale when suddenly the floor gave way sending them into the kitchen below. According to a local newspaper:

"A pianoforte and a heavy wardrobe came down with the debris and owing to the dust and commotion it was some time before help could be rendered. It was then found that several people were most seriously injured."

On June 9th 1888 the same newspaper announced the death of Mrs Sarah Gabbatis of Etton, the wife of a local butcher, who had been injured in the collapse of the floor.

As well as telling us about the importance of farming to the local economy Etton School's logbooks also reveal something of the impact that the Holderness Hunt has had on the village. The kennels of the Holderness Hounds were established here in 1842 and the excitement and employment opportunities that foxhunting provided could be a source of disruption to the children's education. It was with a sense of sarcasm that the schoolmaster wrote on March 8th 1888:

"I let the children leave at 11.30am as the hounds ran close past the school in full cry. Several boys were absent in the afternoon and in consequence they were in 'full cry' the next morning"

The Holderness Hunt continues to operate from Low Hall in the village and the kennels here have also been used since the 1960s by the Hunsley Beacon Beagles. They have around seventy members and hunt

The Hunsley Beacon Beagles being exercised on Chantry Lane. The beagles have kennels at Low Hall in Etton.

on foot from September until March. Following a trail or hunting rabbits and hares with dogs is still within the law.

As well as being the long established home of hunting Etton is also famous locally for its 'Processed Pea' Folk Evenings based at the village pub, 'The Light Dragoon' This began life in 1969 and was the brainchild of four local music enthusiasts. One of these was Etton resident Stuart Bell who came up with the name 'Processed Pea' after being given the task of selling on a huge consignment of tinned peas at work!

In the forty years since its inception the 'Processed Pea' has been the venue for a host of musical talent including national celebrities like Richard Digance. It is the intimate atmosphere of the Light Dragoon with its beamed ceilings and the rapport between performers and audiences that make these evenings so popular.

The downside to the Etton story is that the village no longer has a shop or a village school. Etton Church of England Primary School closed its doors for the last time on December 16th 1966, a hundred years after its opening, and the few remaining children were transferred to nearby

The Light Dragoon Public House has been the home of 'The Processed Pea' Music Evenings since 1969.

Cherry Burton. However the 'Light Dragoon', the village hall and the parish church of St Mary remain to provide important focal points of this thriving rural community.

CHAPTER 28

FLAMBOROUGH

Of all the beautiful places that abound in East Yorkshire one of the most iconic is Flamborough Head, the chalk headland eight miles long that separates Filey Bay and Bridlington Bay. One of the great 'natural wonders' of Yorkshire this promontory and the nearby village of Flamborough have long been places of 'pilgrimage' for those who enjoy walking, bird watching or simply a relaxing holiday by the seaside.

Unlike most East Riding communities where the 'land' was the most important factor in their growth it was the 'sea' that was the major driving force in the long history of Flamborough. The name itself is thought to be derived from the Scandinavian word 'Flan' meaning a spit or tongue of land and the influence of Danish sea-borne invaders from the 9th century can still be seen and heard in local place names and the dialect of the inhabitants. For centuries this isolated peninsula was called 'Little Denmark' and long ago, to celebrate Flamborough's former loyalty to the Danish crown, the Lord of the Manor, in an annual ritual, is said to have shot an arrow carrying a gold coin out to sea.

Surrounded on three sides by high chalk cliffs and with access to the sea limited to two small coves (North Landing and South Landing) Flamborough was once of strategic importance in keeping watch for sea-borne invaders and there was a signal station here in Roman times. The lighting of beacons was a traditional method of warning in times of danger and this may explain the purpose of one of Flamborough's oldest structures: a chalk built octagonal tower from 1674. Seventy-eight feet high and with an iron grill at the top where wood or coal could be set alight the tower is the only example of its type in England.

One of those times of danger came in 1779 when a famous sea-battle took place off Flamborough Head between ships of the Royal Navy and a squadron commanded by the legendary American hero John Paul Jones during their 'War of Independence.' The nearby town of Bridlington had been reduced to a state of abject terror by the exploits of Captain Jones who was known to be cruising off the Yorkshire coast in search of prey. A large fleet of British coastal vessels had sailed into Bridlington Bay seeking sanctuary from Jones and the harbour was so crowded with ships that many had to be chained together on the outside of the piers. Two companies of the Northumberland Militia were stationed in

The purpose of Flamborough's seventeenth century chalk tower remains a controversial subject. Some maintain that it was an early lighthouse while others claim that it was simply a beacon tower.

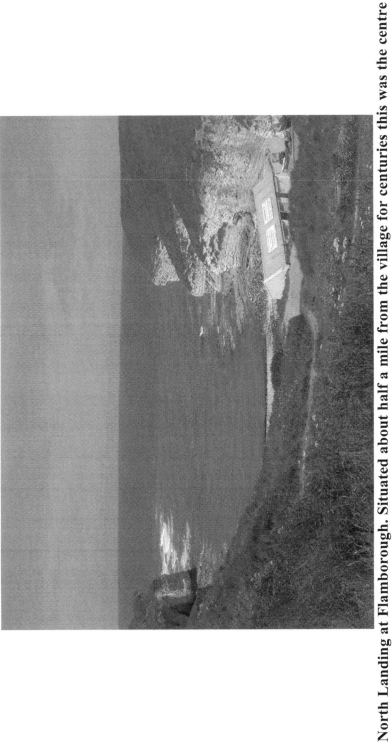

North Landing at Flamborough. Situated about half a mile from the village for centuries this was the centre of Flamborough's fishing industry. In the nineteenth century each crew sold their catch by auction on the beach to local dealers. The fish was then carted by donkey to the cliff top and thence to the railway station at Sewerby. Plans to build a tramway from the cliff top to Sewerby station (1886–1900) came to nothing.

Portrait of John Paul Jones c. 1890 by George Matthews based on an earlier picture by Charles Peale (1741-1827).

the town and local inhabitants who could bear arms were mustered at Bridlington Quay in preparation to repel an expected invasion. Bridlington had every reason to fear an attack since Jones had earlier launched a daring assault on the town of Whitehaven on England's west coast.

In the event Bridlington remained safe from American attack. Instead, on the evening of September 23rd 1779, local people were to hear gunfire out at sea and those who hastened to the cliffs at Flamborough were able to watch one of the most desperate naval battles in history taking place by moonlight. The American fleet of four ships had encountered a Baltic convoy off the Yorkshire coast protected by two British warships. The main interest in the battle off Flamborough Head centred on the duel between the American's 'Bonhomme Richard' commanded by John Paul Jones and the Royal Navy's 'Serapis' commanded by Richard Pearson.

The engagement commenced around 7pm with the two ships firing broadsides at each other. Given the superiority in guns of the 'Serapis', Jones could not hope to win by firepower alone and so he opted for close-quarters fighting and by skilful seamanship he was able to bring the 'Bonhomme Richard' alongside the 'Serapis' by using grappling hooks and lines. There then began a desperate and bloody fight between the crews of the two vessels while the British gunners continued to fire wreaking havoc with the hull and lower decks of the 'Bonhomme Richard'. These were so punched with holes that the sea began to flood in and the ship began to sink.

It was then that fate came to the aid of the Americans. A grenade thrown from the rigging of the 'Bonhomme Richard' exploded near ammunition in the hold of the British ship. In the explosions that followed twenty British crewmen were killed and many more injured. With this disaster the guns of the 'Serapis' fell silent and Pearson was forced to surrender his ship to Jones.

Despite the odds the Americans had prevailed against the superior British ships pitted against them. However, attempts to stop the 'Bonhomme Richard' from sinking proved fruitless and she sank under the waters of the North Sea on the 25th September. Now in control of the 'Serapis' Jones sailed for Texel in Holland and a hero's welcome.

Considered by many to be the 'Father of the American Navy' John Paul Jones and his exploits off Flamborough Head have continued to enthral an adoring American public in the centuries following his death. Such is their interest in him there have been several attempts to locate the

'Bonhomme Richard' on the seabed but so far the wreck has proved elusive.

In the century that followed the Battle of Flamborough Head the population of the village continued to grow and many of its inhabitants earned their living from fishing. Sailing their small boats, or cobbles, mainly from the North Landing there were three types of inshore fishing activity: line fishing for species like cod, crab and lobster fishing and drift net fishing for herring. Some fishermen supplemented their income through smuggling and caves on the north side of Flamborough Head were ideal for storing contraband. Of these caves the largest is 'Robin Lythe's Hole' at North Landing and said to have been named after a smuggler. Many houses in the village had a 'smugglers hole' to hide goods like brandy and tobacco and it was partly to curb the activities of those who attempted to defraud the Customs men of their revenue that a coastguard station was established at Flamborough in the 1830s. Reductions in customs duties in the mid 19th century made the smuggling trade less lucrative but there were still those who were willing to try to outwit the authorities. A local newspaper of September 1884 reported that a Dutch ship described as a 'floating grog shop' had been seen off the Yorkshire coast and that a search of four Flamborough fishermen had revealed "about 28 lbs of tobacco, a quantity of cigars and Eau de Cologne in their possession." The four were charged with smuggling at a magistrates court, pleaded guilty and were heavily fined.

The risks of being caught smuggling were however nothing compared to the dangers of the sea itself as many Flamborough fishermen were to discover. On a fine day the waters around Flamborough Head can look tranquil and safe to the casual observer but in stormy weather the sea can be quickly whipped into a frenzy while razor sharp rocks especially north of the headland add to the dangers. A history of the area records that in 1794 about twenty Flamborough fisherman were drowned in one such storm. A monument on Chapel Street in the centre of Flamborough commemorates another tragedy. On the 5th February 1909 two local fishing cobles: the 'Two Brothers' and the 'Gleaner' returned home during a gale and the rolling waves made the narrow entrance to North Landing hazardous in the extreme. A large roller capsized the 'Gleaner' and in going to the rescue of its crew the second coble also came to grief. An attempt to reach the stricken vessels by the lifeboat Forester was beaten back by the wind and the sea and as a result six fishermen lost their lives in the tragedy.

A photograph of around 1900 showing the volunteers who manned one of Flamborough's two lifeboats.

The dangers of Flamborough Head were not confined to fishermen alone for between 1770 and 1806 one hundred and seventy ships were wrecked here and to improve safety Trinity House was asked to build a lighthouse on the headland. This was constructed by John Matson of Bridlington at a cost of £8000 and first lit on 1st December 1806. Originally conceived as an oil-burning lighthouse it was electrified in 1940 and became automated in 1966.

Although visible twenty miles away the lighthouse alone could not prevent further tragedy. One shipwreck was the steamer 'Caledonia' en route from London to Scotland when it came to grief on Flamborough Head in late February 1864. According to a newspaper report of the time the crew and passengers took to the boats and were saved but the ship itself was dashed to pieces and "the shore strewn with portions of wreck and cargo." Almost three years later a worse tragedy was to follow when a cargo ship called the 'Charlotte' laden with timber from Sweden was wrecked north of Flamborough Head during a snowstorm. The captain and three seamen were found alive among the rocks at the entrance to

Robin Lythe's cave but three others were killed and the captain himself died later from his injuries.

Following an even more catastrophic loss of life during the 'Great Gale' of February 1871, when about seventy seamen perished in Bridlington Bay, the decision was made to establish two lifeboat stations at Flamborough. Situated at the North and South Landings and manned by volunteer fishermen, these gallant RNLI lifeboat crews helped to save many lives in the years that followed. These days the single lifeboat station at South Landing has an inshore Atlantic 85 lifeboat and the nineteen volunteers who operate the vessel continue to give assistance to those in difficulties. Some of these are holidaymakers whose fishing boats break down, children in inflatable craft in danger of drifting out to sea or swimmers who misjudge the perils of strong tides off the coast.

Holidaymakers are now a vital part of the local economy. The attractiveness of the village and the spectacular coastal scenery of Flamborough Head began to attract visitors from the 1890s and helped to counteract the decline of the fishing industry. By 1936 Flamborough had seven refreshment rooms and cafes, a golf course and tennis courts while local fisherman were able to supplement their incomes by taking holidaymakers on pleasure trips.

These days Flamborough is a magnet for those many retired people who have come to love the scenic beauty of the Yorkshire coast. Two hundred years ago Flamborough had a population of about seven hundred people but by the time of the 2001 census this had grown to over two thousand. With its appeal to bird watchers, walkers and holidaymakers it is not surprising that in the summer months the village sees a huge influx of visitors too.

CHAPTER 29

BURTON PIDSEA

One of the major changes to the flat countryside of Holderness in the last two hundred years is the way that meres and marshes have been drained to produce rich cultivable soils. The names of villages can sometimes give clues to how the landscape has been dramatically altered by improved drainage and the village of Burton Pidsea, four miles east of Hedon, is a case in point.

The present-day village name appeared in the 13th century and comes from the mere or lake which once occupied part of the low lying and water logged plain of Holderness close by. Improved land drainage meant that Pidsea Mere had disappeared by the mid 17th century although its name lives on through the village.

A difficult terrain and a circuitous road system probably contributed to a sense of isolation that can still be felt by some visitors to Burton Pidsea today. In the eighteenth century the route to Hull lay via Burstwick, Hedon, Preston, Bilton and Holderness Road making journeys difficult and time-consuming. It is interesting to note that an 1823 directory of the village listed Peter Drew and David Tavender as the village carriers and their horse-drawn wagon had to set off at 4am each Tuesday for the five-hour journey to Hull.

According to the 1823 directory Burton Pidsea had a population of 378 people and had the usual trades of any tight-knit rural community of the time including three shoemakers, two tailors, two blacksmiths and a cabinet-maker. Also listed was Isaac Raines, the village surgeon and apothecary and his medical services in dealing with accidental injuries on surrounding farms would have been vital in a place as isolated as this. It is an indication of his prosperity that in 1818 he built a new residence, Graysgarth House on a two-acre site to the west of the village centre. It was probably this house that was one of those referred to by the local historian George Poulson when he said in the 1840s:

> "The village is luxuriant and picturesque and there are some large and good houses. The timber that surrounds them may be ranked upon the giants of the forest. The soil is rich and fertile and the whole of the parish is in a state of cultivation."

Old cottages in the conservation area of Burton Pidsea.

The Nancy Inn at Burton Pidsea is believed to date from the 18th century and was renamed in the mid nineteenth century in honour of the local racehorse bred by Edward Baxter.

Another of these 'good houses' was 'The Paddocks' owned by Edward Baxter the largest farmer in the village in the mid-nineteenth century. According to the 1851 census Baxter had been born in Burstwick around 1788, farmed 1,500 acres and employed forty-two labourers. Four of these labourers lodged with him at 'The Paddocks' together with a son, a daughter and three domestic servants. Baxter was also an enterprising businessman who owned the village mill and was a brick and tile maker too. It was, however, as a racehorse breeder that he is perhaps best remembered for Burton Pidsea's village pub – 'The Nancy' on Church Street - was named in honour of the horse that brought him remarkable success in the mid-nineteenth century. In 1851 Nancy won eleven races including the Chester Cup and the Ebor Handicap at York and many local fortunes in the East Riding were made on the strength of its success. The horse was based at stables in Beverley and returned home to a hero's welcome with large crowds and the town band paying tribute to its achievements. Baxter's own good fortune and generosity was shown in

Burton Pidsea when he provided five cottages for elderly people, named 'Nancy Row' in honour of the famous racehorse.

The 'Nancy Inn' also served as a village blacksmith's shop and according to a directory of 1857 William Rotsea was working at the forge and serving drinks to thirsty customers. A later licensee of the 'Nancy Inn', Miles Medforth, who in 1892 was described as both a victualer and a shoemaker, continued this tradition of a dual-purpose business. In fact Bulmer's Directory of 1892 listed several other people in the village who combined different trades including Richard Robinson (tailor and shopkeeper), Samuel Cousens (joiner, wheelwright and painter) and William Ford (grocer, draper and postmaster).

Also listed was Mary Brown who ran a private school and the village schoolmistress Henrietta Taylor. The National School in Burton Pidsea had been built in 1860 and was supported by parental contributions, by parish funds and after 1869 by an annual government grant. With an average attendance of around sixty pupils responsibility for the school was transferred to the East Riding County Council in 1909 and they improved both the school buildings and the master's house. During the 1920s and 1930s the school was visited on numerous occasions by the county inspector and his observations provide an interesting perspective on both the school and the village. In November 1922 the inspector wrote:

> "This is not yet one of the best East Riding County Schools. The children are still rather uncouth and their written work is untidy"

In an age when villages in the East Riding relied on wells and pumps for their water his reports also indicate how primitive conditions were for the children and staff. In July 1923 for example the inspector reported:

> "The pump has just been repaired. It is found however that the water has been contaminated and has a bad smell. Seven dead moles were taken out of the well and there is a need to clean it out"

Perhaps influenced by the "grousing" of the headteacher, Miss Barnes, in 1924 the inspector gave the astonishing view that "Burton Pidsea is an awful village to live in."

Three years later the inspector was forced to investigate a parent's complaint about the caning of his son by the headmistress and said:

"Miss Barnes is probably inclined to lose her temper but I cannot believe that she administers excessive corporal punishment. The Mason family do not like Miss Barnes; visits by the School Attendance Officer and the School Nurse have ruffled them. I have however advised Miss Barnes to apply wisdom in her methods of punishment."

Yet looking through the inspection reports for the school this seems to have been an isolated incident and by 1930 the inspector was able to report that Burton Pidsea was " a very satisfactory school."

This is a tradition that has continued into modern times and a 2008 OFSTED report on the primary school said that its "teachers work tirelessly to provide a good standard of education to pupils of all abilities."

The report also paid tribute to the efforts of the school and the wider community to minimise the effects on the school of the disastrous flooding that affected the village in 2007. On the 25th June 2007 Burton Pidsea along with many other places in the East Riding was visited by the greatest catastrophe to afflict the area in modern times: flooding on a huge scale. Following over twenty-four hours of torrential rain that had begun to fall on Sunday 24th June, the drains could no longer cope with the sheer volume of water and streets were turned into raging torrents. The scale of this disaster is indicated by the fact that some one hundred and thirty four houses out of four hundred in Burton Pidsea were flooded including more than thirty occupied by old age pensioners. One of those affected was Brian Sole, a retired sawmill worker who relived the horror of what happened by saying:

"I was looking out of the window of our council bungalow and saw all this water rushing towards us not realising that it was going to hit us at the end of the road. Our home was devastated by two feet of flood water."

It is an indication of Buron Pidsea's indomitable community spirit that volunteers soon turned the village hall into a makeshift evacuation centre and began handing out tea and sandwiches to those evacuees seeking shelter from the devastation. In addition a relief fund was soon launched to help those without any insurance.

The responses of the government and the local authority to the disaster of June 2007 (especially when there were more floods in January

Burton Pidsea Junior School.

2008) remain a controversial issue in Burton Pidsea. Another more recent subject to arouse local anger is that of wind farms for in December 2008 East Riding County Council gave the go-ahead for three huge turbines to be built on a site off Green Lane.

Like many villages close to Hull, which is only eleven miles away, Burton Pidsea has undergone a rapid expansion in the years since the Second World War. With the growth of car ownership it has become a popular commuter settlement and in 2001 had a population of eight hundred and eighty eight people. Large numbers of new houses were built in the 1970s such as the mock-Georgian houses of Barley Garth built in the former grounds of the 'Paddocks' but it retains a recognisable and historic centre from the time when it was still a small and isolated rural community.

CHAPTER 30

LUND

Although many places in East Yorkshire can claim to be the most beautiful in the county few can match the quiet charm of Lund, seven miles northwest of Beverley. The village is set amid the rolling hills of the Yorkshire Wolds and lies to the east of the B1248 road, which effectively by-passes it and allows Lund to benefit from lower volumes of traffic found elsewhere. For those folk who have never seen it, this picture-book village is well worth exploring on foot with the main points of interest being its delightful pond, the magnificent All Saints Church, the village green with its ancient market cross and the nearby 'Wellington Inn' standing adjacent to a former blacksmith's shop.

The origins of Lund probably date back to the Scandinavian invasions of eastern England in the ninth century for the name itself is derived from a Norse word meaning an 'open space in a wood'. The village had a church before the Norman Conquest although the oldest part of the present structure seems to date from the fifteenth century. At the heart of the village in medieval times there was also an ancient hall the home of the Lords of the Manor and rebuilt in the eighteenth century as the Manor House (now Manor Farm). During the thirteenth century Lund obtained a charter granting a weekly market and an annual three-day fair. The fair survived into the nineteenth century for a directory of 1868 records that "a fair for the sale of pedlery is held on the fourth Thursday of Lent."

Most of the buildings at the centre of the Lund date from the early nineteenth century at a time when the village was still essentially an agrarian community. The journalist Edward Baines writing in 1823 recorded that there were fifteen farmers in the parish. Important East Riding landowning families like the Broadleys and the Grimstons also had a powerful influence on Lund. The Grimston Family of Kilnwick, for example, controlled the 'living' at All Saint's Church and chose the vicar there. During the time of John Grimston (1725-1780), an energetic local magistrate, the vicar, William Mosey, sent a number of letters to Kilnwick Hall and these give an interesting perspective on life in the village in the late eighteenth century. These days Lund tends to be a tranquil law-abiding place but the letters of William Mosey, held by the East Riding Archive Service, point to a more turbulent past. Harvest time

All Saints Church at Lund on a spring day with daffodils in bloom. The church has a font dating from 1150 and part of the tower is from the 15th century. There was much restoration work on the church in the 19th century.

Lund's ancient market cross. The stepped base is medieval while the tapered shaft from 1755 replaced an earlier one. A charter of 1295 during the reign of Edward the First granted the inhabitants the right to hold a weekly market and a three-day annual fair. The fair lingered on until the nineteenth century. To the right of the Wellington Inn is Manor Farm, the site of an ancient hall used by the Lord of the Manor in medieval times.

and the gathering together of large numbers of workers brought with it the potential for disorder and Mosey wrote:

> "The disturbances in Lund last Saturday were great and we were happy in having you to discourage them."

During the eighteenth and early nineteenth centuries the policing of East Riding villages depended on a system of unpaid parish constables chosen from the local community and troublemakers could cause serious problems. The people of Lund sometimes looked to local magistrates for support and in 1720 we learn of a petition signed by Robert Watkinson, constable, and sixteen other villagers. The petition asked for help in dealing with Mary Rea "a strong and lusty young woman" who had for several years lived a "wicked and dissolute life not applying herself to any kind of labour." The petitioners charged that Mary Rea lived "by begging, whoring and stealing" and that she was "such a threatening abusive woman that none of our people can live quietly."

By the second part of the nineteenth century the inefficient system of unpaid parish constables had been replaced by paid officers and from the East Riding Archive and local newspapers we learn of more lawbreaking at Lund. In January 1861 Police Constable Thomas Sedgwick visited the 'Wellington Inn' to find that the landlady, Mary Foster, was allowing gambling on the premises. The magistrates told her that they would deal with her leniently because she was a widow and imposed a fine of five shillings (25p) and costs of eleven shillings (55p). However a newspaper report of her trial reveals that Mary Foster did not take kindly to her punishment for "she did not seem in the least to appreciate the forbearance of the bench, but was very noisy and rebellious".

Next to the 'Wellington Inn' stood the village blacksmith's shop and in the nineteenth century the red-hot fire of its forge and the sound of a hammer on the anvil would have been familiar sights and sounds in the village. The village smithy was an essential amenity at a time when horses for transport and farm work had to be shod or agricultural machinery needed repair. The skills of a blacksmith were ones that were often passed on within the family and in census records and local directories of Lund the name 'Teal' figures prominently. A directory of 1857 recorded that George Teal was the blacksmith followed in 1872 by James Teal while in 1891 census returns show the presence of Alfred Teal (born about 1859) his wife Anne, age thirty-one, (born at nearby Middleton) and their two month old son George Teal. According to Arthur Mee, writing in 1941, "Alfred Teal made the anvil ring for sixty three years" until he too was succeeded by another son, also called Alfred, in 1936.

It was this Alfred Teal who was still at work in the 1950s when Lund was 'invaded' by about sixty technicians, cameramen and actors from Ealing Studios involved in location shots for the movie 'Lease of Life'. Some of the filming took place at the Green where Alfred Teal "continued working at his forge despite the fact that the spotlights were focussed just outside." It is indicative of just how insular village life could still be at that time since Alfred Teal told a reporter that he had never seen

The filming of 'Lease of Life' began at Lund on the 21st March 1954. Lund was the setting for the fictional village of Hinton St John. On the right is the director Charles Frend with Robert Donat playing the part of the Reverend William Thorne. (Image courtesy of the East Riding Archives Service)

a film in his life and was unsure whether he would make the trip into Beverley to see this one when it was released.

When filming began at Lund on the 21st March 1954 it brought a host of actors to the village - many of them household names. In the lead role of the Reverend William Thorne was the outstanding theatre and film actor Robert Donat the star of Alfred Hitchcock's 1935 masterpiece 'The 39 Steps'. The sad irony of Donat's performance at Lund was that he was a dying man playing a dying man. In the film 'Lease of Life' Donat played the part of the vicar of the fictional Yorkshire village of Hinton St John who had been told by his doctor that he had only twelve months to live. In real life Donat suffered from asthma and such was the fragile nature of his health that oxygen cylinders had to be kept close by when he was acting. 'Lease of Life' was Robert Donat's penultimate film appearance and his 'breathless' delivery of some lines in the movie are a clear indication of the health problems that were to end his life, prematurely, four years later. For his abilities as an actor, Robert Donat was nominated for an award as 'best actor' for his role in 'Lease of Life' at the eighth British Film Academy awards.

While the focus of the 1950s media may have been on the stars of the film the villagers of Lund also secured employment as paid 'extras'. Among these were David Freear the retired village postman, together with Farmer Walker and his son, who received £2.10 for riding his bike down the street. Central to the story were the parish church and vicarage of Hinton St John and both All Saints Church and Lund vicarage were used to portray the exterior shots. The wife of the real vicar of Lund, the Reverend Lancelot Foster, had already been invited down to London to see the reconstructions of her kitchen, hall and lounge that had been built in the studio. Back in Lund she told a reporter:

> "It is rather like being in a dream. Everything was just as it is here but it was all in a studio two hundred miles away."

One of the interesting features of Lund in the 1950s was that it still had a tailoring business and this became a tobacconist's shop for the purpose of the film. Meanwhile Lund Village Hall served as the canteen for the crew working on the movie.

With the rise of private motoring since the end of the Second World War the village of Lund, like others in the East Riding, has attracted some new housing. However the creation of a conservation area has meant that the heart of this beautiful village has been retained for the enjoyment of future generations. Furthermore, over two centuries there has been a decline in its total population. In the 2001 census the population was just two hundred and eighty nine people whereas in 1823 Edward Baines recorded that three hundred and fifty-seven people lived there.

CHAPTER 31

SKIPSEA

One of the most controversial subjects affecting East Yorkshire in recent times is how to deal with the threat posed by coastal erosion. For centuries Skipsea, along with other places on the coast, has seen its soft boulder-clay cliffs relentlessly eaten away by the power of the sea. Two thousand years ago the coastline lay over three miles to the east and the landscape was very different to that of today. The original location of Skipsea was not as the name suggests by the sea but by the side of an inland lake left behind after the Ice Age. Similar to 'Hornsea Mere', this lake was suitable for both navigation and eel fishing and archaeological evidence from around its shores suggest there was habitation here in both the Stone Age and Bronze Age.

Although Skipsea Mere has now vanished at times of high rainfall, like that of June 2007, parts of the Mere bed are prone to flooding and show us what the landscape used to look like. The name Skipsea (skip saer) is thought to come to us from the Scandinavian invaders of the ninth and tenth centuries and literally means a lake navigable by ships. This mere was connected by a series of channels to the River Hull and probably to the open sea as well.

The defensive possibilities of Skipsea and its lake were recognised at the time of the Norman Conquest by Drogo de la Beauvriere who around 1086 built a motte and bailey castle here to defend the area against Viking raids. The motte or mound of the castle was built on an island in the lake and was linked by a causeway to the shore and to a crescent-shaped bailey covering eight acres and defended by an inner and outer ditch and a rampart. Drogo had fought alongside William the Conqueror at the Battle of Hastings in 1066, was married to his niece and was entrusted by the king with the Lordship of Holderness. However his tenure of Skipsea Castle was not to last long for in 1087 he fled back to the continent because, according to the 'Meaux Chronicles', he had poisoned his wife. Edward Baines writing in 1823 recorded that the spirit of the unfortunate woman was said to haunt the castle and to this day local legend claims that anyone who walks around the mound twelve times at midnight can conjure up the ghost of this 'White Lady'.

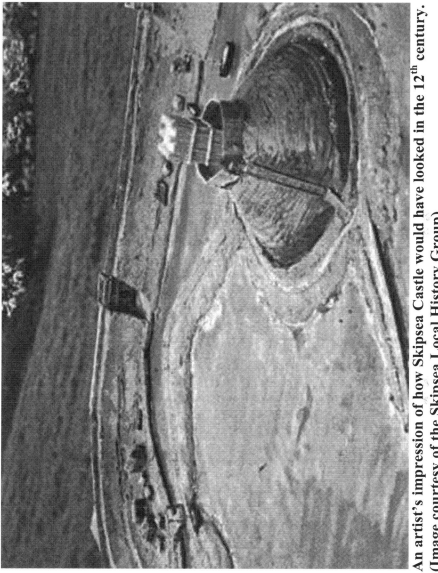

An artist's impression of how Skipsea Castle would have looked in the 12th century. (Image courtesy of the Skipsea Local History Group)

Since the keep and other parts of Skipsea Castle would have been built of wood nothing survives today other than the massive earthworks. In the thirteenth century, another Lord of Holderness, William de Forz II, rebelled against King Henry III and the Sheriff of Yorkshire was ordered, in 1221, to destroy the castle at Skipsea along with William's other castles at Skipton and Cockermouth.

Yet it was the presence and protection of the castle and its importance as the first 'seat' of the Lords of Holderness that provided the initial stimulus to the development of Skipsea. In the 12th century another of these 'Lords', Count William le Gros created a fortified borough close to the castle with houses and shops to provide him with an income from tolls and rents while in 1327 King Edward the First granted Skipsea a weekly market and two annual fairs. However in the long term this community did not prosper to the same extent as other places in the East Riding, such as Hedon, probably because the Lords of Holderness preferred to live at Burstwick rather than Skipsea.

In the centuries that followed life in this remote area of East Yorkshire would have been dominated by the needs of farming and subject to the harsh realities of an existence dependent on the vagaries of the harvest, the weather or natural calamities like the plague and other poorly-understood illnesses. In such circumstances people would often blame misfortune on 'supernatural' causes and in the mid-seventeenth century Skipsea was caught up in the same paranoia about 'witchcraft' that existed in other parts of Britain. In 1650 Ann Hudson of Skipsea was accused of bewitching a neighbour, Susannah Keld, and making her ill. Although such accusations would be considered ludicrous today at the time there was a widespread belief in witchcraft. This was fuelled by growing uncertainties provoked by the English Civil Wars (1642-1648), the execution of King Charles the First (1649), by religious zeal and by the activities of Matthew Hopkins, the Essex 'Witchfinder General' who is said to have sent around two hundred and thirty alleged witches to their deaths between 1645 and 1647.

The trial of Ann Hudson took place at the York Assizes and was based on the information of Dynah Hunmansby and Alice Stevenson given to a local JP on the 4th September 1650 and contained in documents held by the Public Record Office at Kew. They claimed Susannah Keld had told them "twelve years ago" that Anne Hudson had cast a spell to make her ill and that as a result she was "very much tormented and troubled and did languish." It was then alleged that when Ann Hudson had visited Keld in her sick bed the patient had scratched the 'witch' to

217

The Main Street at Skipsea.

draw blood and blunt her 'powers' and that Susannah Keld had then made a full recovery. Superstitious and foolish as this so-called 'evidence' sounds it was probably enough to convict Ann Hudson and we know that numerous 'witches' were executed on the gallows of York Castle. Although it cannot be proved it seems likely that her accusers would have been motivated by malice and the chance to 'settle scores'. After all it had taken them twelve years to come forward with their accusations.

Although we do not know the verdict of the court in the case of Ann Hudson there are other cases involving residents of Skipsea that show how harsh the criminal law could be with wrongdoers in the past. On 17th October 1749, for example, Elizabeth Thrusk was seen carrying away flour, bread, pillows, petticoats and other items from the house of Elizabeth Collinson in the middle of the night. For this felony she was sentenced by magistrates to seven years transportation and she was probably sent to work in the plantations of Virginia.

In the nineteenth century Skipsea, like most other places in the East Riding, was dominated by the needs of farming and a directory of 1857 named twelve farmers along with the usual trades of blacksmith,

The origins of Skipsea Sands Holiday Park can be traced back to around 1951 when a few caravans were established on a field owned by Cliff House Farm.

tailor, joiner and shoemaker vital in such an isolated place as this. The coming of the railway from the mid-nineteenth century had helped other coastal places in the East Riding like Withernsea, Hornsea and Bridlington to develop as seaside resorts but Skipsea was not connected to the rail network and had to wait until the arrival of motoring for its potential to be realised. Holidaymakers started arriving in greater numbers from the 1930s and tents, wooden chalets, caravans, and old railway carriages became a familiar sight near the cliff edge.

The development of Skipsea as a seaside resort gathered pace after the Second World War with the 'Skipsea Sands' Caravan Park being developed from 1951 on farmland belonging to Cliff House Farm. After 'United British Caravans' bought the land in 1954 development continued apace with piped water and electricity eventually being laid on. By the time of the new millennium 'Skipsea Sands' had become a major holiday centre and now has over seven hundred static caravans together with facilities like a heated indoor swimming pool, a sports centre, a bowling alley, a bar and shops.

Another of Skipsea's major attractions is 'Mr Moo's ice cream factory and parlour', a family-owned business based at Southfield House Farm. This was the brainchild of Stephen and Judith Foreman who in 2003 decided to diversify their dairy-farm business and move into the production of high quality dairy ice cream.

Using milk from their dairy herd at Harpham and other quality ingredients Mr Moos has built up an enviable reputation for the excellence of its ice cream and in just seven years production has soared. As well as selling ice cream direct to the public there is also a thriving wholesale business with sales to farm shops, entertainment venues and leading Yorkshire supermarkets.

Other, older, businesses continue to thrive here too including Skipsea Post Office Stores and 'The Board Inn' both at the heart of the village. Another reminder of the past located there is the brown marble war memorial (left) erected in remembrance of those who gave their lives in two world wars. One of the brave Skipsea folk whose name was inscribed on the memorial was Private George Statters, of the fourteenth battalion of the East Yorkshire Regiment who was born in 1876. He died in November 1916 during the Battle of the Somme. His parents lived at Ivy House in Skipsea.

These days Skipsea is a thriving coastal village and has attracted those who want to live near the seaside but want to be near to towns like Beverley and Bridlington. This lovely village also has a remarkable community spirit and thanks to major fund raising efforts by its residents saw the opening of a new village hall in September 2010.

CHAPTER 32

WOODMANSEY

When people think of a typical East Riding village they will often bring to mind places with a specific 'focal point' such as a church, like Skirlaugh, a pond, like Bishop Burton or a village green, like Ellerker. The village of Woodmansey, over two miles in length, is a very different type of East Yorkshire settlement for it is really a collection of communities that lie adjacent to the busy A1174 Hull to Beverley Road. These places include the semi-rural hamlet of Thearne, the commercial hamlet of Plaxton Bridge and the original village of Woodmansey based around King Street. In the last eighty years the distinction between these three 'elements' has been blurred by 'ribbon development' along Hull Road, Ferry Lane and Thearne Lane.

One of the unifying features of Woodmansey's component parts is the low-lying nature of the ground for nowhere does it reach seven metres above sea level. In the past this area close to the River Hull was subject to serious flooding despite the existence of dikes to improve drainage here and it is significant that the name 'Woodmansey' is derived from 'woodman's pool'. However around Thearne and Woodmansey there were patches of boulder clay that helped to raise them a little above the level of the waterlogged carrs close by. The name 'Thearne' is derived from 'thorn tree' and in the Middle Ages there was a 'chantry chapel' here dedicated to St Mary at which prayers were said for the souls of the departed. However making a living here from farming must have been difficult for it was said "Thearne was fit for nothing but frogs and toads." However the land is now much drier than it was. Local tradition says that the area was transformed less than a century ago when a large borehole was sunk at the Dunswell Water Works by Hull Corporation.

Another unifying theme of Woodmansey was the Hull to Beverley Road. This grew in importance as Hull developed as a thriving port from the Middle Ages. The need to keep the road 'dry' is indicated by the writings of the traveller Celia Fiennes who said in 1697:

> "We went from Beverley to Hull six miles all upon a causeway secured with two little rivers running on each side."

The Hull to Beverley Stage Coach.

At the beginning of the eighteenth century maintenance of roads was still the responsibility of the local community but since this labour was unpaid it was either done badly or not at all. Such was the importance of the route from Beverley to Hull that it was the first in the East Riding to be taken over by a 'turnpike trust' in 1744. They were given the responsibility of improving the road but made travellers pay a toll for using it. At 'Toll Barr Cottage' in Woodmansey at the junction of Long Lane and Ferry Lane, a toll-keeper collected money from those joining the road here including those arriving from Wawne Ferry. The tolls varied according to the type of vehicle or traffic using it with a coach or wagon drawn by four horses paying one shilling (5p) and someone on horseback one and half old pence (less than 1p). However one of the complaints of travellers joining the main road at Woodmansey Bar was that they still had to pay the full toll for a limited use of the road.

By the early nineteenth century there were several stagecoaches each week using the route through Woodmansey. Passengers aboard the 'High Flyer' or the 'Accommodation' passing by in 1823 would have seen only a tiny village close to the main road comprising some cottages, farmhouses and a public house called 'The Altisidora'. These were built in and around a cul-de-sac now called King Street.

At the time of the 1861 census one of Woodmansey's residents was farm labourer David Richardson (age 44), his wife Hannah (age 42) and their seven children. At the other end of the social scale was the noted Beverley antiquarian Gillyatt Sumner (age 67) who was described as a "landed proprietor".

Gillyatt Sumner (1793-1875) had bought his house in 1825 and was an avid collector of all things historical. During his lifetime he built up a huge collection of books, manuscripts, deeds, antique furniture, coins and antiquities of all kinds. After his death the whole of this remarkable collection built up over sixty years was sold at an auction lasting three days held at the Assembly Rooms in Beverley (1877). The East Riding Archive in Beverley now holds much of Sumner's valuable legacy and anyone who has used the archive's online catalogue to seek out material on the history of East Yorkshire will have come across references to "volumes assembled by Gillyatt Sumner."

For the poorer residents of the village however life here could be as harsh as it was elsewhere. On the 25th January 1865 the East Riding coroner recorded a verdict of death by starvation on a widow called Eliza Smith (aged 60) from the village. The neighbour who found her told the inquest that Mrs Smith had no food in the house only "some old bones

The Warton Arms with its distinctive thatched roof replaced a 1930s pub called the Dixon Arms.

which had been picked at and an apple or two." The daughter of the deceased told the coroner that in the previous year her mother had applied to the Beverley Poor Law Guardians for relief during the winter but had been refused unless she came into the workhouse. The inquest was told that the widow had refused the offer saying she would rather starve. The coroner suggested that the Beverley Guardians had been "harsh" in not allowing the woman a "few shillings in the winter after she strove to maintain herself in the summer."

In the nineteenth century education was often seen as the way to improve the lot of the labouring poor although much depended on the voluntary effort of local benefactors in providing it. Until 1856 there was no school within two miles of the village but in that year the efforts of the Reverend J B Birtwhistle of Beverley Minster led to the opening of Woodmansey School. Until the construction of the nearby Church of St Peter in 1896-1897 the building also served as the village church.

Situated on a bend of the main road opposite the church is the Woodmansey, Thearne and Beverley Parks War Memorial erected in

Woodmansey School. When it first opened in March 1856 this building served as both a church and a school.

memory of those who gave their lives in the First World War. Among the names inscribed on the obelisk was that of Private Ernest Wise of Woodmansey who served with the sixth battalion of the East Yorkshire Regiment and who died in France in September 1916.

Meanwhile Woodmansey and Thearne School continued to prosper and grow after the First World War and was regularly inspected by East Riding County Council in the 1920s and 1930s. James Affleck had been the head teacher since 1893 and the schools' inspector (Mr J Moffat) after a visit in November 1921 wrote in his rather patronising style:

> "The headmaster is a very nice man of the harmless type. Methods are about twenty years out of date. Mr Affleck is too much fixed in his habits of steady monotonous routine to change now and it will be best at his age to leave him undisturbed."

Hendrik Los and his wife Ivy on a visit to the Netherlands in the 1950s and wearing traditional Dutch costume. (Image courtesy of Peter Los)

Moffat's inspection reports also provide us with evidence of the growth of Woodmansey at this time for between 1921 and 1933 the numbers attending the school rose from fifty nine to ninety seven. The inspector wrote in his report of April 1929:

"Owing to the increase in numbers working conditions are become worse. Building is going on in the neighbourhood and more children are arriving."

The economy of Woodmansey showed remarkable growth in the years between the two world wars with market gardening being a good example. The rich alluvial soils of the area and the proximity of Hull's fruit and vegetable markets had long been a stimulus to market gardening and from around 1935 the industry was given a boost by the arrival of growers from the Netherlands who brought with them superior methods of Dutch horticulture. Cornelius Los and his brothers Marinus and Hendrik were encouraged by a Dutch merchant at Hull's Humber Street Market to settle in the area and they built up a thriving business growing a variety of vegetable and salad crops including tomatoes and cucumbers under glass. In the late 1930s and beyond the Los family were part of a thriving 'Dutch colony' in Woodmansey, Cottingham and Brough.

Today Woodmansey remains a thriving centre of enterprise with the Tokenspire Business Park located at the northern end of the village and a cluster of businesses around Plaxton Bridge including 'Bell Truck Services', 'Welwyn LGV Driver Training' and 'O'Leary Motor Homes'. Woodmansey is also home to two major garden centres within half a mile of each other: the 'Beverley Garden Centre' and the 'Outlet Garden Centre'. 'Coletta and Tyson Limited', one of Europe's largest producers of bedding plants, own the latter. From its headquarters in Hull Road Woodmansey and sites in Thearne, Cottingham and South Cave, Coletta and Tyson has become one of the region's major success stories and supplies plants to a number of famous UK retailers.

The present-day Woodmansey has therefore a great deal to interest those who enjoy exploring the villages of the East Riding by car, by bike or on foot. Those who leave the main A1174 route and explore the quieter byways of Thearne Lane, Ferry Lane, Long Lane and King Street, will encounter a more tranquil world with numerous clues to its fascinating past.

227

CHAPTER 33

BARMBY MOOR

Good communication by road has long been an important factor in the growth of East Yorkshire villages and the position of Barmby Moor close to the busy A1079 road helps to explain the importance of the place both in the past and today. The village grew up at the junction of Roman roads leading from York and Stamford Bridge to Brough and where 'Keld Spring' provided the inhabitants with a plentiful supply of crystal clear water. Although archaeological evidence like coins and pottery suggest there was some settlement here in Roman times the name 'Barmby' is derived from later Anglo-Saxon settlers. It comes from the Norse word 'Barnby' or 'Barnes Farmstead' while the 'Moor' part of the village name is derived from the common land that lay beyond the three arable fields farmed communally until enclosure in the later 18th century. According to a local history of the area Barmby Common was said in 1691 to comprise about a thousand acres and able to support four hundred horses, several hundred sheep and numerous other beasts during the summer months.

Although it is hard to imagine today the desolate nature of the moor made it an ideal place to waylay travellers on the road to York and this was to earn the village a reputation as 'Black Barmby' in the seventeenth century. One of these criminals was twenty three year old Charles Spooner of Bradford who robbed and murdered Francis Groves at Barmby in late 1658. For these crimes Spooner was executed at Walmgate Bar, York on the 29th May 1659 and was taken back to Barmby not for burial but for his body to be put on display in a 'gibbet' by the roadside. A gibbet was an iron cage hung from a gallows-type structure and designed to hold the decomposing corpse of any particularly notorious criminal often for years after their execution. In the macabre language of the time the idea was "that in order to deter others, the punishment should not cease at the place of execution but the body should be suspended between earth and heaven, as unworthy of either, to be buffeted by winds and storms." Spooner was not the first criminal to be displayed in this way at Barmby Moor for in 1603 the same fate befell William Pendleton who was gibbeted for the murder of John Young of Pocklington.

The importance of the main York road meant that it was one of the early ones in the East Riding to be turnpiked (1764) with the Beverley-

The junction of Main Street and Chapel Street at Barmby Moor.

Kexby Bridge Turnpike Trust able to charge tolls on the traffic using the thirty miles within its control. Improvements to the road meant that stagecoaches began to operate every day of the week except Sundays. According to the writer Edward Baines writing in 1823 the stagecoach 'Trafalgar' left York every morning for Hull taking six and a half hours to complete the journey. One of the stopping places was Barmby Moor Inn where travellers could obtain refreshments while the horses were changed. In 1823 Baines said of it:

> "This is a large and commodious inn that has been kept by its present owner and occupier Mr Thomas Heard for thirty-six years. The letter bags to and from Pocklington are received and delivered here."

Yet, in the long run the coaching inn and the traffic that supported it was to suffer from the competition of the railways for in 1840 a railway connection from Hull to York via Selby was opened. The dramatic consequences of this was shown in 1841 when Thomas Hutchinson, who had a lease to collect the tolls at Barmby Moor, applied for the cancellation of his agreement. Meanwhile 'Barmby Moor Inn' without the stimulus of the coaching trade struggled on for another ten years before closing its doors.

By the early nineteenth century the village of Barmby Moor had a population of four hundred and forty people but Pocklington had around one and a half thousand and the arrival of the York to Market Weighton railway there in 1847 seemed to confirm the dominance of Barmby's near neighbour. Pocklington also had a thriving market while Edward Baines reported that Barmby's market had been reduced to a once-a-year event preceding the village's famous annual feast. The official day of the feast was the first Thursday after the 10th July but the festivities usually continued on the Friday and Saturday too. Barmby Feast probably began as a religious festival in the Middle Ages to mark 'St Peter's Day' but by the nineteenth century had developed into a 'fun-filled' event with plenty of eating, drinking, horse races, cricket matches and the like. By the 1920s there was also a fun fair on the village green with swing boats, roundabouts, fortune tellers, shooting galleries and hoopla stalls to entertain those from the village and places further afield. The fun fair today continues to be an eagerly awaited part of the 'Barmby Feast' celebrations. These days a Saturday in mid-July has become the main focus for this ancient festival with the election of a 'feast queen' who

Shown on the right is the 'Barmby Moor Queen' for 2009: Caroline Gardham. On the left is her attendant Vicky Appleton. (Image courtesy of the Barmby Moor Feast Committee)

rides in procession through the village and presents prizes and judges competitions.

Those who have been to the 'feast' in July and to Barmby at other times of the year will know what an attractive village it is with its two greens, its wide grass verges, a beck lined with willow trees, a seventeenth century manor house, and the Church of St Catherine with its distinctive tower and spire. The Church was largely rebuilt in 1850 - 1852 but the tower and spire remain as a testament to the skill of Yorkshire's medieval masons. The graveyard of the church is reputed to be the largest in the East Riding and one section of it contains a number of 'war graves'

St Catherine's Church at Barmby Moor was extensively rebuilt in the mid nineteenth century while the tower and spire date from the fifteenth century.

of military personnel from the nearby airfield. Called Pocklington Airfield, even though it lay mostly within Barmby Moor Parish, its three concrete runways and associated buildings were constructed by Wimpeys from late 1939 and the aerodrome opened in April 1941. Within months it became a base for heavy bomber squadrons of the Royal Canadian Air Force and several of their aircraft were lost during both operational and training flights with significant loss of life. One of these was a Wellington bomber less than a year old that took off on a test flight from the airfield around 9.30 am on the 5th January 1942 during intermittent snow showers. Shortly after take off the aircraft developed mechanical problems and the port engine caught fire. Eyewitnesses said that the aircraft exploded in mid-air as the pilot tried to make a forced landing near Strensall. All five of the crew were killed and were interred three days later at Barmby Moor Churchyard. Another tragedy leading to funerals there took place in July 1942 when a Halifax aircraft returning from a bombing mission over Duisburg, Germany went into a spin and crashed into New Street, Pocklington. The two Canadian pilots and the rest of the crew were killed.

The proximity of the airfield also left Barmby Moor vulnerable to enemy attack and on the 24th April 1941 a German plane dropped a string of seven bombs on the west end of the village causing minor damage. More serious was an incident on Christmas Eve 1944 when a V1 flying bomb exploded within the village damaging the school and thirty houses. Flying glass and debris also injured a small number of inhabitants.

The Royal Canadian Air Force continued to operate from Pocklington Airfield until September 1945 and it has been estimated that that one hundred and fifty of its personnel stationed there were killed in action. The airfield itself ceased to be operational in 1946 and after full closure in 1965 became, in part, an industrial estate. However, the airfield's association with flying is maintained through its use by Pocklington Gliding Club.

Like many other villages in the East Riding Barmby Moor has seen considerable expansion since the Second World War. By 1971 the population was seven hundred and sixty eight and at the time of the 2001 Census the parish population had grown still further to one thousand and sixty five people. Despite the growth in housing Barmby retains a terrific sense of identity and the thriving community spirit here is reflected by the activities at its well-used village hall. With activities like French classes, art classes, pilates, keep-fit, bridge, a toddler group, flower arranging, line dancing and whist there is a great deal in the village to interest all tastes. The village also benefits from the philanthropy of the 'Calley Trust'. This is a charity dating back to the eighteenth century and was originally established for the needy of the village before the days of the Welfare State. These days the trust uses the income from its investments to support a number of village activities including outings for the elderly, the school, the church, the playgroup and the village hall.

While the periphery of the village has seen some new house building in recent years the special character and beauty of its historic centre has been recognised by the East Riding County Council. In 2008 this was designated as a 'conservation area' and in their appraisal of this "loosely built-up village" they said that with its appealing combination of eighteenth and nineteenth century houses, its open spaces, its stream and its mature trees Barmby Moor has "a character that is rare in an East Riding context."

CHAPTER 34

WOLD NEWTON

For those who enjoy exploring the quieter byways of East Yorkshire and the scenic beauty of the Yorkshire Wolds the area north of Driffield has much to offer with a number of pretty villages close to the B1249. One of these is Wold Newton, the most northerly village in East Yorkshire; it can be reached by turning off the main road at Foxholes and heading east for about three miles.

Situated in the valley of the Gypsy Race (a river that runs both above ground and below it) the village is only one of a select number in the East Riding to be considered worthy of conservation area status. With its lovely mere, the open space that surrounds it together with its gradually ascending Front and Back Streets it is not hard to see why this ancient community has a magical quality to it. The Mere, fed by the Gypsy Race, is the focal point of the village with all the roads radiating from it. Those who explore the place on foot will also be able to admire a number of listed buildings including Wold Newton Hall (built 1797-1809), the lovely Norman Church of All Saints and the 'Anvil Inn' which dates from the late 18th century and was once a blacksmith's shop.

Although the name Wold Newton (New Farmstead in the Wolds) comes to us from the Angles, a Germanic tribe who arrived from the 5th century, archaeological evidence shows there was settlement here during the Stone Age and the Bronze Age. In a field on the outskirts of the village is 'Ba'l Hill Long Barrow' and during excavations in 1894 five stone-age burials were found along with artefacts like hand tools were found. The Romans were here too and built a road through the area from Foxholes to Burton Fleming along the banks of the Gypsy Race.

Until the advent of piped water the Gypsy Race, the Mere and several wells would provided the inhabitants with their drinking water but in earlier times waterpower was also used to grind wheat and other food grains into flour. There was a water mill at Wold Newton in the early 13th century and this would have been a vital resource in the centuries that followed when most villagers would have been engaged in communal farming under the open-field system.

Like many other East Riding villages Wold Newton's open fields and common pastures were enclosed in the late eighteenth century and the continuing importance of agriculture was shown by the census returns for

Front Street at Wold Newton shows how the level of the land drops sharply from the Yorkshire Wolds.

Wold Cottage was the gentleman's residence of Edward Topham, a poet, playwright, landowner and magistrate. The building served as both his home and also as a courthouse. There was also a small jailhouse and prisoners would be kept there before being moved to York Castle. These days Wold Cottage provides 'Country Accommodation' for visitors to the area.

the village during the nineteenth century. The 1861 census, for example, tells us that the farmer Thomas Southwell lived at Field House in the village, had 270 acres and employed two labourers and three boys. Living in more humble circumstances in a cottage on Front Street was William Stock, a farm labourer, his wife and two children. Also living on Front Street at the time of the 1861 census was John Summers (wheelwright and joiner), his wife Ann and their two sons Richard and John. John was also a wheelwright / joiner while Richard was described as a 'Turkish Bath Man'. Today Wold Newton is a tranquil place but records in the East Riding Archive show that this was not always so. In 1824 Daniel Simpson, Peter Simpson, Thomas Rickaby and others were charged with 'unlawful assembly' and riot at Wold Newton.

On the other side of the village, on the road to Thwing, stands Wold Cottage: a farmhouse built around 1750 and owned in the late eighteenth century by local magistrate and landowner Edward Topham. It was he who recorded the extraordinary events that were to make Wold Newton famous in the years that followed. During the afternoon of 13th December 1795 during a violent thunderstorm a large meteorite weighing twenty-five kilograms struck the ground in a field near to Wold Cottage embedding itself into the chalk bedrock beneath the soil. Topham's shepherd and a farmhand who were close to the impact witnessed the event. Both swore, under oath, to the truth of what they had seen and based on their testimony Topham wrote:

> "Witnesses that saw it fall agree perfectly in the manner of its fall and that they saw a dark body moving through the air and ultimately strike the ground."

Although the existence of meteorites from space striking Planet Earth is commonplace knowledge today at the time the concept of "stones falling from the sky" was revolutionary. Thanks to Topham's meticulous investigation the existence of 'extraterrestrial' matter became an

established fact among the scientific community. The Wold Cottage Meteorite was the first whose fall was recorded and the second largest ever found in Britain. After it was recovered several collectors and astronomers around the world including the Natural History Museum in London acquired parts of it. Recognising the significance of the event Topham himself erected a brick monument in 1799 (left) at the exact spot where the meteorite landed and visitors to Wold Cottage can still see this today. Indeed the story of Wold Newton's famous meteorite continues to make the headlines with the return of fragments for display in the village becoming well-publicised events.

Wold Newton hit the headlines once more in August 1938. The farming community around the village know that their success can often depend on the vagaries of the weather with storms, heavy rain, unseasonable frosts and drought just some of the difficulties to contend with. A scrapbook of newspaper cuttings in the East Riding Archive in Beverley records how Wold Newton and its farms were devastated by freak weather conditions in August 1938. One report said:

> "The storm broke about 2pm and lasted two and half hours. There was a heavy fall of hail with some snow and motor cars had to be dug out of drifts two feet deep. Heavy hailstones broke windows, poultry and geese were drowned and hedges were swept away. Crops have been ruined and several houses flooded."

One witness to these unusual August weather conditions said that Wold Newton looked "like a little Switzerland" while enterprising coach firms in Bridlington quickly organised trips from the resort so that the curious could see the spectacle first hand. With damage estimated at £5000 an appeal went out to the wider community to help those who had suffered in the disaster and among the claims submitted were those of Montagu Harris of Manor Farm whose losses of barley, oats and root crops were put at £158.

Wold Newton became involved in a major controversy in 1991 when its primary school was embroiled in a 'opting out' disagreement with the local education authority. Changes by the then Conservative government had allowed primary schools to apply for 'grant-maintained' status and Wold Newton, under the guidance of its headmaster, John Wallace, became the first primary school in the country to do so. A 'war of words' then ensued between the headmaster and county councillors and this continued for some years with, in 1996, the council refusing to supply the school with library books.

The downturn in agriculture in recent years has mean that many of Wold Newton's famers have had to diversify into other areas of enterprise and one of the most successful has been the 'Wold Top Brewery.' In 2003 Tom Mellor and Derek Gray established a microbrewery at Tom's farm near Wold Newton using locally grown barley and water from their own bore hole. Now wholly owned by the Mellor family the Wold Top Brewery has been a major success story supplying a range of outlets with their award winning cask and bottled real ales. Among these is 'Falling Stone' bitter: a name inspired by Wold Newton's famous meteorite. The name is also used for the pub in nearby Thwing that is owned by the Gray family.

Tom and Gill Mellor. (Photo Adam Fradgley)

Another of the village's enterprising residents from a farming background is Jacqueline Broadhead who in 2006 founded 'Epicure's Larder'. This business is based at Middle Wold Farm and is devoted to the production of fresh, local, high quality food using sustainable farming practices. Among the products she supplies is an award-winning blue cheese called 'Wold Blimey.'

Although Wold Newton has seen some new house building it retains the same tremendous sense of community from times gone by. These days the school, the 'Anvil Arms' and the community centre (the old Methodist Chapel) are the focal points of this thriving community spirit. The activities that take place here show a huge sense of 'involvement' with, for example, everyone keen to play their part in the 'village in bloom' competition.

CHAPTER 35

LITTLE WEIGHTON

Set at the bottom of a dry valley where several winding roads converge Little Weighton is a typical Wolds village with a long main street of houses dating from the eighteenth and nineteenth centuries and a picturesque village pond at its eastern end. Part of the parish of Rowley, the village name is believed to be derived from 'little dwelling place' and even at the beginning of the nineteenth century it still had only a tiny population. Typical of villages of the time the main occupation was farming supported by the usual trades in any self-sufficient community. In 1823 the journalist Edward Baines recorded the presence of six farmers, a shoemaker, a tailor, a blacksmith and a carpenter. The latter, William Hill, also ran the Black Horse Inn which continues to serve the village in the twenty-first century

As the village slowly grew other houses were built on the road to Rowley, once a village in its own right but which by the beginning of the nineteenth century had shrunk to the size of a hamlet. Its main claim to fame is the Church of St Peter and the nearby Rowley Manor Hotel both very much a part of the Little Weighton of today.

By the 1620s the parish of Rowley had a new minister, the Reverend Ezekiel Rogers. He was a devout Puritan whose strict ideas on the kind of activities that should be allowed on Sundays were at variance with the ideas of the Church of England of the time. In 1619 King Charles the First had authorised that pastimes such as dancing and archery might be practised after church on Sundays and went as far as to order churchmen to read, during divine service, his approval of such activities from a document called. 'The Book of Sports.' In 1638 Ezekiel Rogers refused to read from his pulpit that "accursed book allowing sports on the Lords Day" and was dismissed from his post.

Disillusioned by the practises of the Church of England and seeking religious toleration for their own beliefs Rogers and his followers set sail from Hull on board the ship 'John of London' for America. Here in the early spring of 1639 Rogers and the twenty families accompanying him established the village of Rowley, Massachussetts. These events were marked in 1994 when their American descendents donated a stained glass window to the Church of St Peter. The window depicts Ezekial Rogers, other migrant East Yorkshire folk and the ship they sailed in. In 2008 the

The Church of St Peter at Rowley, Rowley was once a separate village but is now considered part of Little Weighton. Rowley is an example of an East Riding 'depopulated village' and apart from the church and the former rectory (now the Rowley Manor Hotel) little else remains.

The stained glass window at Rowley, East Yorkshire donated by the residents of Rowley, Massachusetts, USA. The window depicts the journey of Ezekiel Rogers and his supporters from East Yorkshire to America.

The Beverley Croquet Club was founded in 1986 and has been playing at Rowley Manor since 1987.

BBC genealogy programme 'Who Do You Think You Are' visited Rowley's famous church in a programme about the super-model Jodie Kidd and revealed that she was related to one of the families that had left Rowley in 1639.

Standing near to the church is the former rectory dating back to the eighteenth century and now the Rowley Manor Hotel, a well-known venue for weddings, conferences and social occasions of all kinds. The extensive grounds of the Rowley Manor Hotel have also been the home, for the last twenty years, of the Beverley Croquet Club.

Down the road from Rowley Manor in a deep cutting stands another reminder of its past: the former Little Weighton Railway Station which is now a private residence. In the late nineteenth century the village played a part in a grand enterprise called the Hull, Barnsley and West Riding Junction Railway. Designed to break the monopoly of the North Eastern Railway in the Hull area and to provide the port with a new dock, work on the new railway commenced in early 1881. Building the line through the hard chalk of the Yorkshire Wolds was both a mammoth and

Little Weighton Station in the 1950s.

costly undertaking and nowhere were the difficulties of construction more evident than in the Little Weighton area, the summit of the railway. To the east of the village a cutting eighty-three feet deep had to be dug while to the west of the station Drewton Tunnel, over a mile long, was driven through the chalk at Riplingham. Navvies using picks and shovels did much of this backbreaking labour and in 1883 there were four thousand of them working on the railway alone. Most lived in camps of wooden huts and the largest of these was at Riplingham close enough to Little Weighton for their children to attend the village school and be taught by the schoolmaster, Charles Lacey.

The life of a navvy was both hard and dangerous with most working from dawn until dusk six days a week. For a fifty-eight hour week they were paid between thirty shillings (£1.50) and thirty-five shillings (£1.75) a week. Navvies had a reputation as hard drinkers and hard fighters and sometimes drunken brawls took place. One of the most serious was at Riplingham in April 1882 when Irish and English navvies attacked each other with crowbars and pick handles. To restore order and quell further trouble four hundred of them were sacked.

The railway finally opened in July 1885 with Little Weighton Station decorated with flags and flowers to mark the event. However this new railway was never a financial success and its short operational life (of less than eighty years) never justified the four and a half years and five and a half million pounds spent in building it.

For the villagers of Little Weighton the railway was a godsend since the journey into Hull took only twenty minutes while during hard winters when roads were blocked by drifting snow (like that of 1947) it was usually possible to keep at least one track open even though the other might be blocked by snow or rock-falls in the Little Weighton Cutting. The ending of passenger services to and from Hull in August 1955 was therefore much lamented by villagers. In 1964 the route closed completely and these days Little Weighton Cutting is used for the dumping of household and industrial waste probably making it one of the most expensive landfill sites in history!

Despite the closure of the railway Little Weighton remains an attractive proposition and increasing car ownership since the Second World War has led to new houses being built in the village, such as those in Potterdale Drive and Southwold. One of the major attractions of living there is an excellent village school with glowing tributes paid to it in the December 2007 OFSTED inspection report:

> "Standards are consistently above average and pupils of all ages and abilities achieve well. The school is particularly successful in the teaching of writing and has an excellent track record of pupils reaching high standards in writing."

The school moved to its present site in 1969 and before that classes were taught in the old school on Rowley Road (built in 1873 and now converted into private houses). Education has long been strength of living in the village as revealed by the East Riding Schools' Inspector Mr J Moffat whose reports from the 1920s and 1930s make interesting reading. In 1922 he wrote:

> "Although the teaching is a little old-fashioned it is very good indeed of its kind. Written work is decidedly above the average. Mr Lacey is conscientious and methodical but the infant teacher is weak."

The infant teacher was Miss Bowring and years later Moffat was still complaining about her teaching. On July 18th 1928 he wrote:

The former school house at Little Weighton opened in 1873 with the school bell still visible.

"The infants are very poorly prepared. Miss Bowring, I feel sure, tries her best but her results are far from satisfactory. Teaching is lifeless and uninspiring. She is really inefficient. Unfortunately an invalid mother relies upon her salary."

Charles Lacey was probably one of the longest serving headmasters in the East Riding and was in post for over forty years. Described as "a man of rather attractive personality" who was "handicapped by his staff", it was his teaching of the older children that made Little Weighton in Moffat's words "a good county school"

Little Weighton's popularity as a commuter settlement for Cottingham, Beverley and Hull meant that by the time of the 2001 census it population had grown to over one thousand people. Today its impressive primary school lies at the heart of a thriving community for the village has several organisations like a gardeners' club, a bowling club and a women's association, while other residents are enthusiastic members of the Beverley and District Motor Club.

CHAPTER 36

LEVEN

Motorists heading east from Beverley along the A165 in the direction of Hornsea or Bridlington will probably have seen the village of Leven signposted at the 'White Cross' roundabout. In times gone by the village suffered from the congestion caused by holiday traffic but today it benefits from the by-pass opened in 1994.

Like many East Riding communities in the last fifty years Leven has undergone a rapid expansion with much new house building to cater for those who seek the benefits of country life but who commute to work in Hull or Beverley. In the 2001 census Leven had a population of 2,240 but two hundred years earlier when Britain's first census was taken there were only 411 people living there.

The origins of Leven are in fact much older with the earliest part of the village, called 'Little Leven', dating back to the time of the Ancient Britons although nothing remains of that period today. Yet it is from the nearby River Hull that the village probably acquired its name for *Leven* is thought to be derived from an Anglian word meaning 'the slow moving one'.

According to the Domesday Book of 1086, the Manor of Leven was given by King Edward the Confessor to the Church of St John at Beverley and the manor remained in their hands until it reverted to crown ownership in 1547. There then followed a succession of owners until, in 1742, it was bought by Hugh Bethell of Rise. The Bethells were substantial landowners in the East Riding and the eighteenth century records of the Leven Manor Court indicate their importance to the village. This court dealt with property matters and from court rolls held by the East Riding Archive Service we learn that in October 1745 Anne Simpson was ordered to pay to the Lord of the Manor a yearly rent of one shilling and sixpence (7½p) for her land.

In common with other East Riding landowning families the Bethells were also interested in expanding their business interests and saw the commercial possibilities of investing their money in water-borne transport. The late eighteenth century was an age of canal building and fortunes were being won and sometimes lost, in new canal schemes. In 1799 the newly widowed Charlotte Bethell asked the experienced canal engineer, William Jessop, to undertake a survey for a three-mile canal to

The Leven Canal today. After 1935 the canal gradually fell into disrepair but these days the area is popular with walkers and nature enthusiasts.

link the village of Leven with the River Hull. In March 1800 he estimated that a canal could be built for £4,041 and the following year Charlotte, at her own expense, secured an act of parliament to allow the work to commence. In an age of business dominated by men the enterprise of Charlotte Bethell in promoting her own canal must be unique.

It seems that the Leven Canal cost more than intended for in 1805 Charlotte Bethell obtained a second act of parliament allowing her to increase the tolls she could charge on shipments of coal, corn, lime and other merchandise. At the canal head in Leven was "a commodious wharf and warehouse" where vessels of up to 85 tons could be unloaded. The Leven Canal remained in commercial use from around 1804 until 1935 and the trade generated by it seems to have stimulated the economy of the village for by 1841 the population had grown to 890. One of the new businesses, located close to the canal, was the 'New Inn' where in 1857 Richard Sanders was the licensee and he was also carrying on a range of other activities including that of a corn and coal merchant. At the other end of the village the licensee of the 'Hare and Hounds', Frederick Winter, was described as a "rope, twine and sheep netting maker." Rope making was still a small-scale, labour intensive industry in the mid nineteenth century using 'ropewalks' where yarns of hemp were twisted together between revolving sets of hooks up to 300 yards apart.

The growing economic importance of Leven by the mid-nineteenth century may have been a factor in its choice as a centre of justice. Until that time policing in the East Riding had relied on a centuries old system of unpaid parish constables chosen from local communities. Naturally the job of acting as a constable without pay was highly unpopular and some tried to avoid it often at the risk of falling foul of the law themselves. In 1755 for example we learn of the indictment at the East Riding Quarter Sessions of George Atkinson of Leven, yeoman, for neglecting his duty as constable.

In the early 1850s the authorities in the East Riding came under pressure to improve rural policing and Leven was one of ten places chosen as locations for new 'lock-up houses'. Plans for the Leven 'lock-up' built on High Stile in 1852 however went far beyond a simple police station for this substantial building also housed the magistrate's court of the North Holderness Petty Sessions and responsible for dispensing justice across a wide area including places like Hornsea, Brandesburton, Skirlaugh, Skipsea and Routh.

The plans and specifications for the new building which was constructed at a cost of £654, were drawn up by the renowned railway

Leven's Old Police Station was built on High Stile in the village in 1852 and housed three cells and a courtroom used by local magistrates. The building was built to designs produced by the architectural practice of G T Andrews in York. It is now a doctor's surgery.

architect George Townsend Andrews, famous for his design work on East Yorkshire's railway stations including Paragon Station in Hull. These plans (held by the East Riding Archives Service) show that in addition to the magistrates room there were three cells for prisoners on the ground floor and living accommodation upstairs for the police inspector or his men. The 1891 census records some details from that time: living at the Leven Police Station was Inspector William Cooper, age forty, his wife Clara and their six children.

Local newspapers record the details of many cases of petty crime that were heard by magistrates sitting at Leven Police Court. In October 1900, for example, a local man called Marmaduke Wildman appeared there to answer a charge of cruelty to a horse. The magistrates were told that he had used a lame horse to pull a cart laden with coal and since he

Leven in common with most East Riding villages had a number of trades to support a rural economy. In 1892 the village had three bootmakers, two saddlers and two blacksmiths. Shown here is Fred Turner (1842-1909) outside his forge in the village. (Image courtesy of the East Riding Museums Service)

had twenty-seven previous convictions they fined him one pound including costs.

The Leven Police Station remained in use until 1976 and then became a doctor's surgery- a use that continues to this day. Another old building in High Stile that has been adapted to modern day living is the old boys school built by voluntary subscription in 1873 and these days home to Leven's acclaimed 'Old School House Restaurant'. In fact the village continues to be a thriving centre of business and has a pharmacy, two beauty salons, a butchers/ bakers shop, two public houses, a takeaway and a small supermarket. Leven is also home to some impressive recreational facilities and these include a sports hall on the outskirts of the village provided by the Leven Playing Field Association. Built in 1972 the Sports Hall is the base for a football club, a cricket club and a bowls club. In fact Leven is unusual in that it has two bowls clubs for around 1930 a bowling green was laid out alongside Leven's recreation hall in East Street.

The village of Leven today. This is the original Beverley to Bridlington road through Leven. In the eighteenth century most of the buildings in the village stood along East and West Streets.

Another thriving organisation to be found here is the Hull Aero Club based at Leven Airfield and reached via a rather tortuous and bumpy un-made road to the west of the village. The Hull Aero Club began life in 1929 at the newly opened Hedon Aerodrome in the early days of aviation. On the 11th August 1930 they played host to pioneering aviator Amy Johnson during her triumphal homecoming after her solo flight to Australia.

The airfield at Leven is in fact their fifth 'home'. They moved here from Brough in 1991 and now have about a hundred members. Teaching people to fly and helping them gain their Private Pilot's Licence forms an important part of the club's activities and income. With its welcoming clubhouse, aircraft hangars and its grass runway complete with airsock the airfield is an interesting place to visit.

In the twenty-first century therefore the village of Leven has grown far beyond its rural roots and is a place well worth exploring to explore its beauty, its heritage and its modern-day attractions (including

Peter Haughton and Nuno da Silva of Hull Aero Club at Leven Airfield.

its pubs). For those interesting in walking, for example, a well-signposted footpath close to the New Inn takes you to the canal that two hundred years ago was a major stimulus to the growth of this fascinating East Riding community.

CHAPTER 37

GARTON-ON-THE-WOLDS

With the advent of the 'motor-revolution' of the later twentieth century places in the East Riding that were once only rural backwaters gradually became much busier. Today the main street of Garton-on-the-Wolds lies on the well-used A166 route from York to Driffield and many drivers passing through the village heading for the coast only gain a brief impression of the beauty of the place. A much better way to appreciate the charms of Garton, its conservation area and its outstanding Norman church is to linger awhile and explore it on foot.

The name Garton comes to us from the Angles, a Germanic tribe who settled in the area from the fifth century but archaeological evidence shows that there was settlement here in the Iron Age. One of Garton's major claims to fame was the discovery in 1971 of the chariot-burial of a Celtic warrior. Excavations revealed the body of a thirty-year old man with the wheels of his chariot laid alongside him, the remains of a whip and portions of a pig's head thought to have been buried with him as food for the after-life. Other discoveries included a Roman-style house dating back to the second or third century AD and an Anglian cemetery containing two groups of graves: one pagan and the other Christian.

Like many other places in the East Riding profound changes in land ownership came to Garton with the Norman Conquest. The Domesday Book (1086) shows the estates around the village were now owned by William the Conqueror's brother, the Count of Mortain, and by the Archbishop of York. It is perhaps an indication of Garton's importance in Norman times that it was soon to have a magnificent church. 'St Michael's and All Angels Church' on Station Road is one of the finest and most visited churches in the East Riding. It was established by Kirkham Priory and was built from around 1132. The nave and the tower of the church date from the twelfth century with additions in the fifteenth century and extensive restorations and improvements in the nineteenth century. This work owed much to the generosity of the Sykes family of Sledmere. Sir Tatton Sykes, the fourth baronet, (1772-1863) employed the renowned architect John Loughborough Pearson to restore the church (1856-1857) while his son, the fifth baronet (1826-1913) employed another famous architect of the day George Edmund Street to complete the work. It was this Sir Tatton Sykes, the fifth baronet, who

Garton's beautiful Church of St Michael and All Angels dates from the 12th century. The top belfry stage of the tower was added in the 15th century and the church was restored and beautified by the Sykes family in the nineteenth century.

One of the lovely murals that adorn the walls of the church. The paintings were completed in 1876 at a cost of over £3000.

paid for the beautiful religious frescoes that adorn the walls of the church and that make Garton's church such a popular visitor attraction in the East Riding. Completed in 1876 at a cost of over £3,000 the paintings have been restored in recent years through the efforts of the Pevsner Memorial Trust.

Local newspapers provide a valuable record of village life in the late nineteenth century and twentieth centuries and Garton-on-the-Wolds had its share of crimes, deaths, scandals and accidents to report. Petty crime was a mainstay of newspapers like the Driffield Times and in August 1861 it told its readers that Joseph Hides a shepherd of Garton had assaulted Jeremiah Shepherd a groom living in the same village. Local magistrates fined him one shilling (5p) for the assault with costs of 12s 6d (around 63p in today's money).

More tragically the newspaper recorded a child death in its edition of June 15th 1872. John Elvidge, age six, had become sick on the 4th June and his mother told an inquest that on the following day the boy suffered fits and died. A local doctor attended the inquest and his evidence reveals the poor state of medical knowledge at that time for he said that the child had suffered previously from "congestion of the brain" (probably epilepsy) and that this would have made him liable to a second attack.

The village shop at Garton dates from the early eighteenth century. The impressive bow fronted widows were probably added in the Georgian period.

In March 1900 villagers were shocked to read about the "Garton Bigamy Case" at York Assizes. In July 1883 Emma Duffield from Garton had married Henry Manterfield, an engineer, and he had lived with her in Hull until 1897. The following year he went through a "form of marriage" with Isabella Vine a Leeds nurse even though his first wife was still alive. At a time when divorce was difficult and expensive bigamy was quite common and living in Leeds Henry Manterfield perhaps expected that his crime would go unnoticed. Unfortunately for him Emma Manterfield uncovered his secret, went to Leeds and "created a disturbance in the street" outside his house.

In the months leading up to the First World War Garton residents were shocked by another child death this time the result of a tragic accident. In April 1914 a two-year old boy, Richard Wilson was knocked down by a traction engine travelling down Garton's main street towards Driffield. Richard's father and grandfather were both traction engine drivers and the inquest heard that the boy was "attracted by them" and had run out into the road. The engine driver told the coroner that the front wheel had run over the boy's leg crushing the left thigh. After listening to this and medical evidence the inquest jury recorded a verdict of accidental death.

By the late nineteenth century most of the land around Garton, along with the manorial rights, was owned by Sir Tatton Sykes and his continuing generosity to the village was shown when he rebuilt the village school in 1891. Garton Church of England School had originally been built in 1843 to serve the hundred or so children of this largely agricultural community. By 1921 there were eighty-nine children on roll taught by the Headteacher, Mr Stainer and his two assistants. Mr J Moffat, the East Riding Council inspector, described the school buildings as "very satisfactory" although he was critical of the "unsanitary" toilets. His early impressions of Stainer, who had been at Garton for twenty-two years, were mixed:

> "The Headmaster appears to be a worker and up to date. However his voice is rather rasping and he tires one somewhat by his loquacity."

In his usual blunt manner Moffat later reported on the ill health of Mr Stainer who had several periods of absence between 1923 and 1926. Rather unsympathetically Moffat wrote on the 28th October 1926:

> "Mr Stainer still acts as an invalid, teaches with his overcoat on and for most lessons is seated all the time. I gather from his conversation that he is not likely to apply for a breakdown allowance."

By this time Stainer was fifty-three years old and despite his determination to continue as the headmaster Moffat assumed that he would retire and so 'glossed over' the school's obvious weaknesses. In May 1928 he wrote:

> "The teaching is dull but since the headmaster is nearing retirement it is probably best to allow him to continue."

In fact Mr Stainer did not retire until the end of 1933 and on 5th October of that year Moffat was still complaining of a "tired, lazy atmosphere about the school."

Following Stainer's retirement Moffat's critical comments about Garton School, its new headmaster Mr North and an assistant, early-years, teacher continued unabated. During a visit on the 12th February 1934 Moffat wrote:

> "Miss Davison is a very weak teacher who is self conscious, timid and unintelligent. Her class control is poor"

In the period leading up to the outbreak of the Second World War the inspector continued to visit Garton School and report on the weakness of Miss Davison and on Mr North's "nebulous" teaching style saying, in January 1937:

> "Mr North is inclined to play with toys when teaching of a solid kind is needed."

Under the 'old-style' school inspections of the past Garton School, like others in the East Riding, was able to 'hide' its weaknesses since the reports written about the school were confidential. Since 1992 the Office for Standards in Education has promoted more openness and 'accountability' in its inspections with parents able to view OFSTED findings online. Garton has risen to the challenge and in January 2010 an OFSTED inspection was complimentary about the school, its pupils and their achievements. The report said:

> "Pupils make good progress because they are well taught. As a result, standards are above average at the end of Year 6 in English, mathematics and science."

Garton-on-the-Wolds, like other East Riding villages, has seen considerable change since the Second World War with the disappearance of many trades that were commonplace a hundred years ago. Bulmer's Directory of 1892 shows that in late Victorian times Garton had two wheelwrights, two tailors, a boot maker and three grocers. In the twenty-first century the village is fortunate in that it retains both a shop and a pub. The shop on Main Street retains many of its original features and the building dates back to the early eighteenth century. In days gone by farm workers from Sledmere used to walk there to buy their provisions on the day they were paid.

The main street at Garton forms part of the busy A166 route from York to Driffield. Manor Farmhouse (Kirk View) on the right is a Georgian dwelling and dates from the mid eighteenth century.

With the downturn in agriculture newer enterprises help to keep Garton alive and these include Crispian's Fitted Furniture based at Cedar House Farm Business Park and making high quality handmade furniture and sliding wardrobe systems. The business park itself was the brainchild of local farmer Tim Ewbank who in conjunction with the Crown Estate converted farm buildings into simple, low cost workspaces. Another thriving business based there is 'The Golf Box' supplying a range of personalised and customised tees, balls and other golf-related products.

One of the usual trades found in East Riding villages until the 1960s was a blacksmith and the red-hot fire of his forge and the sound of his hammer on the anvil were commonplace in agricultural communities like Garton. The village is now unique in the East Riding in retaining the services of a blacksmith for at the Garton Heritage Forge master craftsman John Crossland continues a tradition dating back centuries.

The forge has a long history and was built in 1803 by John Dalton. These days it specialises in decorative steel and ironwork like fences,

260

John Crossland, blacksmith, works at the Garton Heritage Forge.

gates, balconies, railings, and staircases and also much smaller items like decorative nails and latches. This highly skilled work is much in demand for conservation 'projects' undertaken by English Heritage and other organisations and from those who simply want to give an 'old feel' to new property.

At the time of the 2001 Census, Garton had a population of around three hundred people. Like many other villages in the East Riding a good proportion of them have chosen a rural lifestyle in which to live and from which they commute to work in places like Driffield, Beverley and Hull. When you take the time to explore Garton-on-the-Wolds with its open spaces, its lovely duck pond and its ten listed buildings you can readily understand the appeal of this beautiful village.

CHAPTER 38

BEEFORD

Those who regularly use the busy A165 route from Beverley to Bridlington will have good cause to remember Beeford, which is eight miles east of Driffield, for its thirty-miles-an-hour 'zone' is regularly policed by a mobile speed camera in a van parked near the junction with the B1249 route. In fact the 'lay-by' it uses was once the main road for until 1936 motorists had to negotiate two sharp bends in the village as shown by old Ordnance Survey maps. These maps can be found on the 'East Riding Archive Maps' internet site and are useful in revealing details of the village a century or more ago and helping us to understand where the name 'Beeford' came from. It is thought the name is derived from 'by-a-ford' for in the days before bridges the roads into and out of the village were crossed by streams like Beeford Beck and these can be seen clearly on the 1910 map. Before the road was straightened these maps also show a village green at the junction of the roads leading to Bridlington, Driffield and Skipsea. A mid-nineteenth century history of Beeford recorded:

> "On the village green is a round-house or lock-up, for misdemeanants, and near it the Stocks – those all but obsolete relics of bygone times may still be found standing in primeval dignity."

Beeford has a past dating back to Anglo-Saxon times and was mentioned in the Domesday Book. In 1086 it was recorded that its English lord had been ousted at the time of the Norman Conquest by one of the followers of William the Conqueror, Drogo de la Beauvriere. In the early eleventh century Beeford was clearly a place of some importance for it had a church and a priest although the oldest part of the present-day Church of St Leonard only dates from around 1240. The tower of the church was added two centuries later and there was some rebuilding and restoration in the eighteenth and nineteenth centuries. In the chancel of the church is a brass effigy of one of its former rectors, Thomas Tonge, who died in 1472.

As well as caring for the spiritual needs of the villagers the medieval church exerted a powerful influence over their everyday lives

The busy A165 Beverley to Bridlington road at Beeford.

too. The Knights Hospitallers at Beverley, an important religious order, were lords of the manor of Beeford from 1316 until their suppression during the reign of Henry the Eighth. As in most East Riding villages until recent times the lives of those living there would have been dominated by the needs of farming and the tasks associated with the changing seasons. A major change came in 1768 with the 'enclosure' of the open fields, the moors and the pastures into compact farms. A number of new brick-built farmhouses, such as that at Alton Farm, were erected in the late eighteenth century and survive today to remind us of Beeford's rich agrarian past.

Twenty-six farmers were named in a directory of 1823 and they would have employed many other 'landless labourers' from Beeford's population of around 623 people. Local farmers would have recruited their workers at the hiring fair called the Beeford Sittings held each November until around 1900.

For those unable to work due to factors like ill health or old age the 'poor law' required the parish authorities to make arrangements for their support. There was a 'poorhouse' at Beeford housing up to four paupers between 1812 and 1815 while others received support called 'out-relief'. The parish authorities, or vestry, were anxious that any unmarried mothers in receipt of parish relief should reveal the name of the child's father so that they could be compelled to pay for their offspring. An entry in the Beeford Vestry minutes in July 1822, for example, said:

> "Jane Latis to be taken before the magistrates to be sworn to the father of her bastard child. She says she has obtained a situation but wants clothes and requests the vestry to sanction her being supplied with them as she cannot otherwise enter her situation."

A month later the minutes showed that the woman's claim that she had a job was "pretence" and that she was once again seeking parish assistance. It was perhaps with some relief that in February 1823 they recorded that Jane Latis had obtained an apprenticeship. The minutes said:

> "Agreed that Jane Latis be bound apprentice it being with her own consent to William Adamson of St Mary's Beverley and to be supplied with necessary clothes."

Beeford Windmill when it had two sails. This tower mill replaced an earlier post mill in 1820. It continued in use until around 1925. (Image courtesy of Mr. K.Warkup and the East Riding Museums Service)

The vestry agreed to meet the cost of £4 10s 0d (£4.50) involved in "binding her apprenticeship" and the cost of the clothes perhaps believing that it would be cheaper in the long run.

After the passing of the New Poor Law of 1834 the use of the 'workhouse system' became the preferred way of dealing with paupers and Beeford became one of the forty-three parishes of the Driffield Poor Law Union. A new workhouse was erected at Driffield and an entry in its 'Register of Births' (November 1901) records how Annie Jane Staveley of Beeford gave birth there to an illegitimate daughter called Mary.

In the nineteenth century directories and census returns show that Beeford supported a number of trades typical of a large farming community of the time like shoemakers, tailors, blacksmiths and wheelwrights. The 1881 census shows the presence on Main Street of Francis Robert Wharram a tailor employing two men and one boy apprentice. Wharram was twenty-five years old and unmarried so he also made use of the services of a housekeeper.

Less typical was the trade of watchmaker and census records from the period 1881 to 1901 provide us with some details. Before the advent of mass-produced wristwatches after the First World War craftsman-made silver pocket watches were in vogue for timekeeping, as an important 'fashion accessory' and as a store of wealth that could be pawned in times of hardship. From the 1881 census at Beeford we learn of Jonathan Watson a fifty-seven year old watchmaker who had been born in Beverley. Shortly after the census was taken Watson died at Driffield in December 1881 but Edwin Postill, a watchmaker from Hull, arrived to take his place. A letter in the East Riding Archive seems to indicate that Postill had a lax attitude towards his children's education for in March 1889 he was warned about the irregular school attendance of his son James, aged eleven. The letter said:

"unless the boy is sent to school regularly application will be made to the magistrates for a summons."

By the time of the 1891 census Edwin Postill still had four children to support. One of these was George Henry Postill, age six and four years later the child was the victim of a vicious assault at Beeford in August 1895. A fellmongers assistant, John Hastings, appeared in court charged with the crime and by way of excuse said that the boy had been in his garden stealing apples. Edwin Postill gave evidence and told the court of his son's injuries including a serious head wound. Other witnesses said that they had seen Hastings strike the ten year old and convinced by the evidence the court declared that he "had committed an assault of a disgraceful nature and had beaten the lad in an unmerciful manner." Thereupon Hastings was fined £1 plus costs and was told that he faced twenty-one days in Hull Prison if he did not pay. The crime,

A silver pocket watch with a white enamel dial. This watch of 1890 was made by 'Barnby and Rust' of the Market Place in Hull. Pocket watches were the 'norm' until the twentieth century and were often attached to clothing by a chain. Seen as a fashion statement they were often produced from a waistcoat pocket with an ostentatious 'flourish'. (Image courtesy of Peter Croton)

however, may have had longer-lasting repercussions for the child and his family; the 1901 census said that George was now an "imbecile" and "subject to fits". By 1901 Edwin Postill's family had grown again and the census shows that as well as sixteen-year old George he was supporting six other children aged between three and fourteen.

Watchmaking and other trades that once made Beeford such a bustling place have now disappeared although farming is still a vital part of the local economy with local firm 'ACMC' a world leader in the field of pig genetics. The company supplies genetically advanced breeding stock to farmers as far away as China. Another village success story is the 'Garth Partnership' on Straight Lane who specialise in pig health management through its veterinary team and have won international renown for their work.

Since the 1960s Beeford has seen considerable growth with new housing estates being built and with its population growing to over one thousand people. John Smith, born in 1927 and formerly the owner of a village shop, told me of some of the changes he had witnessed in his lifetime.

"When I was young there was no piped water and many people had to carry what they needed from a communal pump on the village green. Electricity did not come to the village until 1934 so before that we used paraffin lamps and candles. The village had no sanitation and so people had privies with a bucket under the seat. When that was full they buried the contents in the garden."

The Tiger Public House stood next to the old Bridlington road through the village.

While village businesses like a cycle repairer, a saddler and two blacksmiths have vanished others have continued. The Tiger public house was mentioned in a directory of 1823 and continues to serve the people of the village and elsewhere today. The Tiger Public House stood next to the old Bridlington road through the village and in the late nineteenth century was the scene of a tragedy. In 1891 Emma Nicholson the wife of the landlord was killed in an accident in the pub yard. A local newspaper said that they had been out for the day in a pony and trap but as she tried to get out "the pony gave a sudden start. She was then thrown to the ground upon her head, and died."

A year later a Beeford directory shows that the village had three public houses: 'The Tiger', 'The Black Swan' and 'The Ship'. In 1892 Henry Edwards was the licensee of the Black Swan but by the time of the 1901 census William Lawty, from Winteringham in Lincolnshire, was the innkeeper. Living with him there was his wife Mary, who was from Skipsea Brough and his twenty-three year old son and a nineteen-year old daughter. These days the pub, rebuilt in a mock-tudor style, is called the 'Yorkshire Rose'.

St Leonard at Beeford dates from the thirteenth century.

In the nineteenth century Beeford was described as 'long and straggling' and at around a mile in length remains so today. Yet clearly it is a very desirable place to live for in 2003 it topped a poll commissioned by a leading Sunday newspaper to find the best-value place in Britain to live. On the basis of house prices together with factors like education, health and low-crime rates Beeford beat off competition from elsewhere. With amenities like a butcher's shop, a post office, a doctor's surgery, a vet's practice and a community centre Beeford remains a thriving Holderness village.

CHAPTER 39

PAULL

For anyone unfamiliar with East Yorkshire the village of Paull, about six miles east of Hull, might seem like one of those isolated 'back-of-beyond' places commonplace in this area of Holderness although it has become a familiar sight to passengers heading into Hull on the cruise ships of P&O ferries. Reached by a minor route from the Saltend roundabout on Hedon Road these days the skyline around Paull is dominated by the nearby giant BP petrochemical complex with its vast array of metallic stacks and pipes.

The origins of Paull are however very old and the name of the village and its alternative of Paghill, probably comes from the Angles a Germanic tribe of the fifth century who settled here and possibly means a 'stake' marking a landing place. Like other places on the Humber shoreline ferry boats operated from here to Lincolnshire in the Middle Ages and it was alleged in the mid fourteenth century that the ferrymen at Paull had been taking excessive fares. At a time when sea-going ships were small, Paull also acted as a port and in 1322, for example, during the Scottish wars Paull merchants sent supplies north to assist in the campaigns of Edward the Second.

Paull's links with the sea are also apparent from its famous lighthouse and maritime activities like shipbuilding and, in the past, fishing. The lighthouse close to the Humber shoreline was built in 1836 by Trinity House as an aid to navigation for ships leaving Hull. The lighthouse only had a short operational life and was replaced by other lights further down river around 1870. Now a private residence the lighthouse is supposed to be haunted by a female ghost.

In 1769 the manor of High Paull was bought for £6,700 by Benjamin Blaydes a prosperous Hull merchant and shipbuilder and it was he who built High Paull House. The Blaydes family grew wealthy on contracts to build ships for the Royal Navy and they established a shipyard at the southern end of the village. During the Napoleonic Wars in 1812 a seventy-four-gun ship for the Royal Navy, the 'Anson', was built at the shipyard at a cost of £140,000. It is said that in 1808 the keeper of the Humber Tavern was trying to attract visitors from Hull to the village with promises of being able to see the work in progress at the shipyard and the opportunity to use a bathing machine!

This drawing from the early nineteenth century shows High Paull House. It was built by Hull merchant and shipbuilder Benjamin Blaydes who was twice Lord Mayor of Hull. The house is now demolished but the gatehouse survives.

Paull's famous lighthouse was built in 1836 by Trinity House as an aid to navigation for ships leaving Hull. It is now a private house.

In the early twentieth century Paull had a thriving fishing industry. Shown here is a Paull shrimper.

These days Paull's shipbuilding tradition continues at the Hepworth Yard at the northern end of the village and which builds and repairs fishing vessels, tugs, small ferries, tanker barges and all types of small workboats. Established in 1946 the shipyard is now wholly owned by the well-known local company of J.R. Rix and Sons and its facilities include a large fabrication shed where the hulls of vessels are built and a dry dock used for the fitting out of new vessels.

Paull's other main industry: fishing for shrimps has now disappeared but was a thriving trade in the late nineteenth century as the census of 1881 for the village shows. Living on Paull's main street fronting the river were nine fishing families including that of Robert Dickinson, age 41, his wife Fanny and their four children. The youngest of these was Frederick, aged seven, and twenty years later the 1901 census shows that he was continuing the family tradition by working as a fisherman. Local resident Alice Markham writing of these times recalls that most of the men wore navy blue jerseys and sea-boots while a local history of Paull records that in 1912 there were nineteen men working thirteen boats from the village.

Census records also provide us with information on another of Paull's important features: the battery of guns commanding the approaches to Hull that existed here at various times from the sixteenth century to the twentieth century. The area is generally low lying but south-east of Paull is a deposit of gravel that forms a low riverside cliff and this proved to be the best place to establish a fort for protecting the growing port of Hull from foreign attack. King Henry the Eighth in 1542, established the first Fort Paull but the site took on a new significance in July 1642 with the events leading to the English Civil War. The sympathies of Hull lay with Parliament and so King Charles the First established a battery of guns to fire on any parliamentary ships making their way upriver with supplies. However this battery only had a short life after being bombarded into submission by the Parliamentary ships 'Lion' and 'Employment' and in the process doing damage to the Church of St Andrew situated on higher ground about a quarter of a mile from the village.

A succession of different forts have stood on the same site during its long history, manned at times of emergency, like the Napoleonic Wars and abandoned at others. However in 1854 at a time of growing tension with France the decision was taken to establish a new permanent fort at Paull that would be much larger than its predecessors and with a close proximity to the deep-water channel along which any ships attacking Hull would have to pass. It is this Fort Paull built largely of brick but covered with earth to help absorb incoming bombardments that still exists today. Improved and strengthened in the years that followed the fort stretched two hundred metres along the river, covered seven acres and was equipped with nineteen canons. The 1881 census shows that the Paull Point Battery now had a permanent garrison of troops including Frederick Madden, age 35, a gunner with the Royal Artillery.

With the closure of the Paull Point Battery in the years after the Second World War the complex faced a bleak future until it was 'rescued' by the vision of Brian Rushworth. Brian was a Beverley businessman who was looking for a new challenge and heard about a "strange and mysterious fortress" at Paull in 1989. He told me:

> "When I initially set eyes on the Fort it presented a sad picture of neglect and dereliction. The whole of the site was strewn with rubbish and completely overgrown with vegetation. In spite of this I could sense the magic and history contained within its mighty walls and secret labyrinths."

The entrance to Fort Paull Museum. A fort has stood on this site since Tudor times. The present fort dates from 1864 and was called Paull Point Battery.

Together with a dedicated team of volunteers Brian set about restoring Fort Paull to its former glory with the idea of creating a museum there. It was a mammoth undertaking to clear the site of vegetation and free underground chambers of sand deposits and it took twelve years before the museum finally opened its doors to the public in July 2000. Great care had to be taken with the restoration since the fort is a scheduled ancient monument and there are still underground rooms and passages awaiting excavation.

Since this award-winning museum opened visitor numbers have grown steadily and Fort Paul now brings in over 50,000 guests each year. One of the great attractions of a visit to Fort Paull is the chance to explore its Victorian defences for much of the complex lies below ground. There is a multitude of underground rooms, bunkers and tunnels and descending the various stairways adds to the eeriness and excitement of a place that during two world wars played an important part in the defence of the Humber. As one of the museum staff, Phil Rochester told me:

One of the museums most important exhibits is this Blackburn Beverley transport aircraft.

" During the Second World War the fort was a degaussing station. During the winter of 1939 the Germans began to drop magnetic mines in the Humber. The job of the Wrens based at Fort Paull was to degauss (or demagnetise) ships using electrical cables laid in the river bed so that they would not attract these mines."

The fort with its underground chambers was also well suited to be an arsenal of shells and other munitions much of them destined for the Russian convoys sailing out of Hull.

Some of the large guns on show around the site are on loan from the Royal Armouries in Leeds but other exhibits have come from a wide variety of sources. Cannons built at a local foundry in the nineteenth century and a defused Second World War bomb unearthed at a Hull factory are just some of these. Brian Rushworth told me:

"The offer of items seemed to come faster and faster once we opened. A good example was a twelve-pounder cannon which a

276

diver found somewhere off Spurn Head. He rang us to ask if we wanted it."

A more recent acquisition for the museum is a Hawker Hunter jet fighter that for many years stood at the entrance to the Humbrol factory on Hedon Road in Hull. The aircraft had been a symbol of the 'Airfix Models' side of Humbrol's business but when the factory closed down it was moved and now stands in what was once the parade ground of Fort Paull. Also here is the museum's largest exhibit: the world's only surviving Blackburn Beverley transport aircraft. This famous plane was built at Brough in East Yorkshire and was formerly owned by the Beverley Army Transport Museum. However when this museum closed in 2003 Fort Paull secured the aircraft in a sealed-bid auction. Dismantling and moving the aircraft was no easy task and part of the airframe had to be lifted by heavy crane over the walls of the fort. However thanks to the hard work of volunteers this historic aircraft was on show again from 2005 and today's visitors can marvel at its sheer size and learn about its history from displays inside.

Today the village of Paull, like many others in the East Riding, has attracted newcomers who were drawn to live here by its riverside location but found that it was also a convenient place to commute into Hull. New houses like those on Ferryman Park have helped to swell the population of a village to around eight hundred people. During my visit to the village I spoke to Harold Beadle who has lived in Paull for over eighty years and can remember when, in the 1920s and 1930s the place consisted of just one main street. Reminiscing about the changes to the village in the time he has lived here he said:

> "When I was a boy the village had three shops but no electricity, no gas and no piped water. People had to fetch their water from the village pumps. One of these pumps was in Turpit Lane."

His memories of those primitive times are confirmed by reports in the East Riding Archive. A visitor to Paull School in 1921 said of the toilets:

> "The out-offices are the worst I have seen in the East Riding. The boys' urinal is 'eastern' in its filthiness. This is due to the fact that after school hours the villagers have access to the playgrounds.

Paull's long tradition of shipbuilding continues at Hepworth's Shipyard. Now owned by J. R. Rix and Sons the yard continues to build and repair tug boats, small tanker ships and similar vessels. A recent ship built by the Hepworth Shipyard for the Holyhead Towing Company undergoes trials. (Image courtesy of J. R. Rix)

This cannot be prevented as there is a public pump in the Boys' Yard."

Those 'bad old days' are now just a distant memory for those few residents who can still recall them and Paull folk today can enjoy many of the same amenities that make village life elsewhere in the East Riding so attractive. This ancient community with its old lighthouse, its welcoming pubs, its magnificent views over the Humber Estuary and the award-winning visitor attraction of Fort Paull is a village well worth seeing.

CHAPTER 40

ANLABY

Like many villages close to Hull the growth of Anlaby was closely associated with the development of its much larger neighbour. In the area around Anlaby from the 1930s there was a growing enthusiasm for suburban life and with it came pressure from developers to build houses on green field sites or on the gardens and estates of the grand houses of earlier times. In 2001 the population of 'Anlaby with Anlaby Common' parish stood at 9,883 and the place had taken on the dimensions of a small town. Yet mid-nineteenth century Ordnance Survey maps of Anlaby show the village as a small unique entity far to the west of Hull with fields separating it from places like Willerby, Kirkella and Swanland. In 1800 the population of Anlaby was around 300 people while a gazetteer of 1872 showed that there were now 493 people and 103 houses.

The evidence shows that the Anlaby story began in the late ninth century with the Danish invasions of eastern and northern England. There is a local tradition that settlement commenced around the year 867 with a Viking warrior called 'Anlaf' and the important local family called 'Anlaby' may have been descended from him. Another name long associated with the village was 'Legard' for Robert de Legard arrived there at the time of the Norman Conquest. The village was included in the Domesday Book of 1086 when its name was 'Umlouebi' and through marriage to an heiress of the Anlaby family, around 1100, the Legards secured the lordship of the village for the next eight hundred years.

The connection between the growth of Hull and the village of Anlaby was one that existed from medieval times for Hull, built on 'salt soil', depended on Anlaby for its fresh water from springs like Julian Well. This was to lead to disputes between the two and in 1376 a royal enquiry was ordered into a Hull scheme to make a ten-foot wide freshwater dike from Anlaby alongside the road to supply Hull's growing population. This 'Julian Dike' was in use by the early fifteenth century but the ill feeling continued with in, 1578, a dispute between Hull Corporation and Christopher Legard of Anlaby over the problem of preventing land water from contaminating the spring water in the dike.

The Legard Family lived at the Manor House and old maps of the village show its original thirteenth century location, 'Moat Hill'. In the seventeenth century the Legards were to play an important part in the

The post mill at Anlaby was built around 1657 and demolished in 1909. (Image courtesy of the East Riding Museums Service)

Charles I is refused entry into Hull.

quarrels between King Charles the First and Parliament culminating in the Civil War of 1642-1646. In April 1642 Christopher Legard, a senior officer in the Hull Garrison, was one of those who decided to deny the entry into Hull of Charles the First. Soon after Royalist forces occupied the Manor House at Anlaby and prepared to use it as a base to lay siege to the walls and gates of Hull. However the defenders had made this task more difficult by opening the sluices and breaking down the banks of the Humber in order to create a barrier of flooded land two miles wide.

In the event it was the Royalists at Anlaby who found themselves under attack. On the 27th July a force from the Hull garrison using rafts to negotiate the flooded ground launched a surprise night attack on the

281

Manor House and the royalist munitions stored at Moat Hill. An account of the action said:

> "Captains Loweringer (of the Navy) and Legard (of the army) sallied by night and avoiding the highways by using portable bridges they came three miles from Hull. Making a stand with 40 horse and some 200 foot they fell into Anlaby. They left alone the corps du guarde, took all the rest between sleeping and waking, surprised the sentinel (whom they slew), hurt some others, and carried 12 or 13 prisoners away."

The royalist forces then withdrew to York but they were back in August 1643 when the Duke of Newcastle's army laid siege to Hull for a second time. As with the first siege Hull's defenders chose to take the fight to their enemies by launching another assault on Anlaby. This time however the Royalists seemed to have been better prepared and the assault was beaten off with at least twenty members of the Hull garrison being killed and others being taken prisoner.

In the century after the Civil War Anlaby would have remained a small quiet place dominated by the needs of farming and other rural occupations. One of the factors that restricted development in the early eighteenth century was the state of the roads for maintenance depended on a system of unpaid statute labour. Among the complaints made was that the Hull-Anlaby-Hessle road despite being part of the important route to the West Riding was often made impassable by flooding. To improve this vital road to the west a turnpike trust was established in 1745 with tolls being charged on road users. At the eastern side of Anlaby was Grove Lodge, the tollhouse where money was collected from those joining the road there.

Better communications led to a desire of Hull's well-to-do to move out into the East Riding to enjoy the advantages of country living and Anlaby was one of the locations they chose. In 1823 Edward Baines was able to record "Anlaby is a pleasant village adorned by several elegant seats." Among the six "gentry" he listed in his directory of that year was William Voase who lived at Anlaby House, a late eighteenth century mansion built by John Boyes, a Hull merchant. The Voase family had also settled in Anlaby around that time with John Voase, a Hull wine merchant, living at 'Beech Lawn'. Voase family memorials in St Peter's Church, built in 1865 and restored and enlarged twenty years later, show their importance in the village.

The stable block and water tower at Tranby Croft.

Probably the most famous of Anlaby's mansions was Tranby Croft built around 1874 for Arthur Wilson a member of a highly successful Hull shipping family. The 'Wilson Line' was founded by Thomas Wilson (1792-1869), a merchant in the Swedish iron ore trade who had bought his first ship in 1825. The company prospered under his

House guests at Tranby Croft at the time of the Royal Baccarat
Scandal. Seated in the front row third from the right is the Prince of
Wales and left of him is Lieutenant Colonel Gordon-Cumming.

sons Charles and Arthur and by the early twentieth century the Wilson Line had become the largest privately owned shipping company in the world with over one hundred ships. A local directory of 1892 described Tranby Croft as a "handsome modern mansion of white brick with stone dressings" and the estate had a carriage drive almost a mile long and gardens covering thirty-four acres. The house was one of the first to be lit by electricity, had a lofty tower with an engine and a pump to supply the place with water and a private swimming bath "for the use of all on the Tranby estate."

The 1891 census and directories of the time are particularly revealing about the staff needed to run such a large establishment. Living at the Tranby Croft stables was coachman Frank Lessiter together with five grooms while at the main house the needs of fifty-four year old Arthur Wilson, his wife, two sons and four visitors were met by twenty-three servants. These included a butler, a cook, five housemaids and three laundry maids while taking care of the education of Clive Wilson, Arthur's fourteen-year-old son, was school governess Maria Paulus.

Arthur Wilson was by 1892 a man of considerable wealth and stature in East Riding society for he was now High Sheriff of Yorkshire, a Justice of the Peace and the Master of the Holderness Hunt. However in the 1890s his name and that of Tranby Croft became associated with embarrassing revelations in the press about the 'Royal Baccarat Scandal'.

In September 1890 Wilson played host to the Prince of Wales (the future king Edward the Seventh) during Doncaster Race Week. For evening entertainment the Prince and other guests took part in a game of baccarat at Tranby Croft but one of the players, an army officer called Sir William Gordon-Cumming, was observed cheating (8th September 1890). The following night he was seen to do the same again and six of the guests after conferring with the Prince of Wales confronted him about his un-gentlemanly behaviour. Although Sir William initially denied any wrongdoing he eventually agreed to sign a confession in return for a promise that the affair would be kept secret. In the event the scandal became widely known among the upper classes and fearing that his honour would be irreparably damaged if he did not take action Sir William sued the original accusers for slander in the civil courts claiming that his confession had been made under duress (June 1891).

Since the case involved a member of the Royal Family the proceedings were widely reported in the newspapers of the time. Two of the defendants were Arthur Wilson's son and his daughter-in-law. Much to his embarrassment the Prince of Wales was called to give evidence and while he admitted that he was not playing at the time and had not witnessed any cheating by Sir William he did give this damning opinion about his former friend:

> "That the charges made against him were so unanimous that I had not any other course open to me but to believe them."

The trial ended on the 9th June with the jury taking only ten minutes to find the defendants not guilty. The results for Sir William's career and his social standing were catastrophic because for a 'gentleman' to be found cheating at cards was an unpardonable sin. He was dismissed from the army and withdrew to his Scottish estates never to re-enter high society. Arthur Wilson himself was left untainted by these events but according to one obituary at the time of his death in 1909 the 'Tranby Croft Baccarat Scandal' had such a profound effect on him that he declined a peerage and "saw very little of society afterwards."

Today Tranby Croft is the home of one of East Yorkshire's most prestigious independent schools: the Hull Collegiate School founded in 2005 as the result of a merger between Hull High School for Girls and Hull Grammar School. The former had begun life in 1890 at Albion Street, Hull, with Arthur Wilson being the largest shareholder in the company that promoted it. Hull High School moved to Tranby Croft after the Second World War.

Important local families of the past like Legard, Voase and Wilson are still remembered in the street names of today even though Anlaby has changed out of all recognition to the quiet country village they knew. The huge growth of new properties is shown by plans held by the East Riding Archive with housing estates like South Ella (1935), Mill Lane - Tranby Lane (1959) and Grange Farm (1962) being created. New opportunities for recreational activities like swimming also developed with the opening of the Haltemprice Leisure Centre in 1974 while to this day the village centre retains an impressive range of shops and services including a butchers, a greengrocers, a bookmakers, a post office and a supermarket.

The East Riding Development Plan of 1960 had a profound impact on the commercial growth of Anlaby too for a large number of firms moved into the industrial area north of Springfield Way in the years that followed. Although some of these, like the printing company of Harlands of Hull, have gone there have been exiting new retail and warehouse developments there in recent years including a huge William Morrison superstore.

Other Yorkshire History books from the Blackthorn Press are available as paperbacks or ebooks.

Roman Yorkshire, Anglian York, Viking Age Yorkshire, Early Tudor Yorkshire, Yorkshire in the Reign of Elizabeth I, Yorkshire in the 17th Century, History of Driffield, History of Northallerton, History of Ryedale, History of Selby, History of Scarborough, Scarborough's Heroes, Rogues and Eccentrics, History of Richmond, History of Hornsea, History of York, History of Whitby, History of Filey, History of Seamer, History of Pickering, History of Beverley, History of Thornton-le-Dale, Villages of East Yorkshire, The Story of York, The Story of Hull, The Story of Bradford, The Story of Pickering, Marston Moor, Adwalton Moor, Yorkshire in the Civil Wars, Whitby Pickering and Scarborough Railway, Sir Hugh Cholmley, The Rowntree Family of York, J R Mortimer, The Yorkshire Mary Rose, Religion in Yorkshire, Francis Nicholson, Victorian Ships, A Fine Eye for Colour.

English Literature from the Blackthorn Press includes:

D H Lawrence: Complete Short Stories, Complete Travel Writing, Complete Plays, Complete Essays, Complete Novellas and all the novels. Wilfred Owen Complete Poems, William Wordsworth Selected Poems, Brontë Sisters Selected Poems, Truth is Not Sober, Trollope Complete Short Stories and many other titles available as paperback or ebook.

All these and other titles are available from our website www.blackthornpress.com or from the Amazon website.

Printed in Great Britain
by Amazon